Late Nineteenth-Century American Diary Literature

Twayne's United States Authors Series

David J. Nordloh, Editor

Indiana University at Bloomington

TUSAS 524

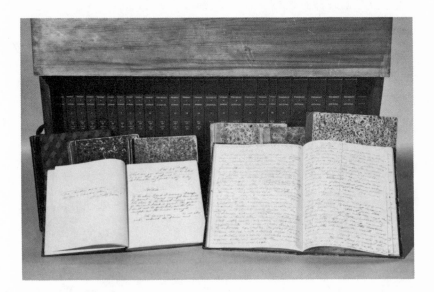

The Journals of Henry David Thoreau
Photograph courtesy of the Pierpont Morgan Library

Late Nineteenth-Century American Diary Literature

By Steven E. Kagle

Illinois State University

Twayne Publishers
A Division of G.K. Hall & Co. • *Boston*

Late Nineteenth-Century American Diary Literature
Steven E. Kagle

Copyright 1988 by G.K. Hall & Co.
All rights reserved.
Published by Twayne Publishers
A Division of G.K. Hall & Co.
70 Lincoln Street
Boston, Massachusetts 02111

Copyediting supervised by Lewis DeSimone

Book design by Barbara Anderson

Typeset in 11 pt. Garamond
by Compset, Inc. of Beverly, Massachusetts

Printed on permanent/durable acid-free paper
and bound in the United States of America

Library of Congress Cataloging in Publication Data

Kagle, Steven E.
    Late nineteenth-century American diary literature.

    (Twayne's United States authors series ; TUSAS 524)
    Bibliography: p.
    Includes index.
    1. American diaries—History and criticism.
2. American prose literature—19th century—History
and criticism.   I. Title.   II. Series.
PS409.K33   1988   818'.403'09   87-17734
ISBN 0-8057-7504-8 (alk. paper)

For Jonathan and Matthew

Contents

About the Author

Steven E. Kagle is Professor of English at Illinois State University, where he teaches colonial and nineteenth-century American literature, creative writing, and science fiction literature. He received an A.B. degree in English from Cornell University and holds an M.A. in English and a Ph.D in American Culture from the University of Michigan.

In addition to this volume, Professor Kagle is the author of *American Diary Literature 1607–1800* and *Early Nineteenth Century American Diary Literature*. He is the editor of three books: *The Diary of Josiah Atkins* (New York Times and Arno Press, 1975), *Plymouth* (by Carol Gesner, published by *Exploration,* 1976), and *America: Exploration and Travel* (Popular Press of Bowling Green University, 1979). In addition he is the author of a number of shorter works; among these are several dealing with diary literature, including "Diary of John Adams and the Motive of Achievement" (*Hartford Studies in Literature,* 1971), "Diary as Art: A New Assessment" (*Genre,* 1973), and entries in *American Writers before 1800* (Greenwood Press, 1983) and in *Dictionary of Literary Biography: American Literature of the Revolution and Early National Period* (Gale Research, 1985). For ten years he served as editor of *Exploration,* a scholarly journal on the literature of travel and exploration.

Preface

This book, the third in a series of works on American diary literature which I have written for the Twayne United States Authors Series, marks the end of a long project. The first book in this series, entitled *American Diary Literature 1607–1800,* was published in 1979 and the second, *Early Nineteenth Century American Diary Literature,* in 1986. When I began this project twenty years ago I was one of only a few scholars working on American diaries as literary works. Even though scholars had long since accepted the importance of the genre to American literature, little had been published except as part of studies with another focus.

Today, the situation has greatly changed. A number of studies have been published or presented, and the number is growing. I do not know to what extent my books have helped in this development, but it has been my intention in writing them to open this rich body of literature to future scholarship. I have only been able to cover a small number of the diaries worthy of study. Some of the diaries I have studied have never before been considered in print, and I do not presume to have had the last word on any of those I treated. In "The American Scholar" Emerson wrote that no book should be seen as the final word on a subject because the "right use" of any book is "to inspire." My greatest wish for this work is that it may make this vast and varied body of literature sufficiently manageable that others will find it easier to apply their talents in reading and studying it.

While the subject of this volume is the diary literature of the second half of the nineteenth century, not all of the material covered here fits exactly between the first moment of the year 1850 and the last of 1899. Neither human lives, cultural movements, or literary trends break so conveniently according to the arbitrary divisions of the calendar. Many diaries span such dividing lines, and others are appropriately part of movements the major portion of which fall in a different period. For example, Hawthorne's notebooks start in 1835 and Charles Francis Adams's diary in 1820; however, the most important part of each of these works is at or after mid-century. Bryant's and Colton's both conclude before 1850, but both deal with the settlement of the West Coast which was just beginning.

Steven E. Kagle

Illinois State University

Acknowledgments

I am indebted to the following institutions and their staffs for permission and assistance in using the libraries and other facilities: the American Philosophical Society, the Boston Public Library, the Eastham Public Library, Harvard University, Haverford College (especially the staff of the Quaker collection), Illinois State University, the J. Pierpont Morgan Library, the Library of Congress, the Newberry Library, the New Jersey Historical Society, the New York Historical Society, the New York Public Library, the Pennsylvania Historical Society, the University of Illinois, the University of Wisconsin at Madison, and Yale University.

I am grateful to the following individuals and institutions for permission to quote from works to which they hold the rights:

The Adams Manuscript Trust for the microfilm edition of *The Adams Papers* (1954).

Cherokee Publishing Co., Atlanta, Georgia, for *The Wartime Diary of a Georgia Girl, 1864–1865* (1960).

Dodd, Mead & Co. for *The Diary of Alice James* (1964).

Harvard University Press for *The Diary of Charles Francis Adams* (1964) and *The Journal of Richard Henry Dana, Jr.* (1968).

The Historical Society of Pennsylvania for *A Philadelphia Perspective: the Diary of Sidney George Fisher Covering the Years 1834–1871* (1967).

Excerpts from *The Heart of Burroughs's Journals* edited by Clara Barrus. Copyright 1928 by Clara Barrus. Copyright renewed 1956 by Adeline Barrus Johnson. Reprinted by permission of Houghton Mifflin Company.

Ho for California! Women's Overland Diaries from the Huntington Library (1980) reprinted with the permission of the Henry E. Huntington Library.

Indiana University Press for *A Confederate Girl's Diary* by Sarah Dawson (1960).

Louisiana State University Press for *Brokenburn: The Journal of Kate Stone, 1861–1868* edited by John Q. Anderson, copyright 1955.

Reprinted with permission of Macmillan Publishing Co. from *The Diary of George Templeton Strong* edited by Allan Nevins and Milton

Halsey Thomas. Copyright 1952 by Macmillan Publishing Company, renewed 1980 by Milton Halsey Thomas.

Michigan State University Press for *Army Life in a Black Regiment* (1960).

The Modern Language Association for *English Notebooks* (1962).

Ohio State University Press for *The Centenary Edition of the Works of Nathaniel Hawthorne*, including *The American Notebooks* (1972) and *The French and Italian Notebooks* (1980).

Oxford University Press for *Writing Nature* by Sharon Cameron (1985).

Henry D. Thoreau, *Journal*, Vol. 1: *1837–1844*, ed. Elizabeth Hall Witherell. Copyright © 1981 by Princeton University Press. Henry D. Thoreau, *Journal*, Vol. 2: *1842–1848*, ed. Elizabeth Hall Witherell. Copyright © 1984 by Princeton University Press. J. Lyndon Shanley, ed., *Walden: The Writings of Henry D. Thoreau*. Copyright © 1971 by Princeton University Press.

Ross & Haines Inc. for *What I Saw in California* (1967).

R. R. Donnelly & Sons for *Private Smith's Journal* (1963).

University of Chicago Press for *Journal of Benjamin Moran 1857–1865*, ed. Wallace and Gillespie, copyright 1949 by the University of Chicago Press.

Russell T. Schwarz, Executor, for *Mollie: The Journal of Mollie Dorsey Sanford in Nebraska and Colorado Territories 1857–1866* (1959).

W. W. Norton & Co. for *Memoirs of a Volunteer* (1846), *The Journal of Charlotte Forten, a Free Negro in the Slave Era* (1981) and *The Diary of Gideon Welles*.

Yale University Press for *Mary Chesnut's Civil War*, edited by C. Vann Woodward, © 1981 by Yale University Press.

I am also grateful to the following libraries for permission to quote from documents in their collections: the Houghton Library of Harvard University for the manuscript journals and diaries of Thomas Wentworth Higginson; the Library of Congress for the Benjamin Moran Papers; and the Historical Society of Pennsylvania for the manuscript of *Diary: December 1848–March 1849* from the George Mifflin Dallas papers. In addition I would like to thank the J. Pierpont Morgan Library and its staff for their assistance and permission in securing the photograph of Thoreau's journals used as a frontispiece for this book.

I would also like to acknowledge the aid of my graduate assistants, Price Flannigan, James Baran, Chanpen Hantrakul, and Tipa Thep-

Acknowledgments

Ackrapong, and the support of Illinois State University for research grants that helped me to complete this work.

Finally, I would like to thank my wife, Jill, and my sons, Jonathan and Matthew, for their assistance and encouragement.

Chronology

1849   Walter Colton describes the beginning of the California Gold Rush.

1850   George Templeton Strong goes to hear Jenny Lind.

1851   First publication of Daniel B. Woods's *Sixteen Months at the Gold Diggings.*

1853   Nathaniel Hawthorne becomes American Consul at Liverpool and begins his *English Notebooks.*

1854   Publication of Henry David Thoreau's *Walden,* a work developed from his journal.

1856   George Mifflin Dallas becomes minister to the Court of St. James.

1857   Helen Carpenter leaves by wagon train for California.

1858   Mollie Dorsey records her engagement in her diary.

1859   Charles Francis Adams begins his term in Congress.

1860   John Beatty serves in the electoral college that elects Abraham Lincoln.

1861   The start of the Civil War drives Judith McGuire from her home in Virginia.

1862   Charlotte Forten goes to teach freed slaves in the Sea Islands of South Carolina.

1863   Benjamin Smith fights in the battles of Lookout Mountain and Chattanooga.

1864   John Ransom writes of the suffering in Andersonville.

1865   Gideon Welles describes the death of Abraham Lincoln.

1868   First publication of Hawthorne's *American Notebooks.*

1870   Thomas Wentworth Higginson publishes his revised diary, *Army Life in a Black Regiment.*

1871   Worn by illness and financial problems, Sidney George Fisher dies.

1872   Bronson Alcott publishes *Concord Days* in diary form.

LATE 19TH-CENTURY AMERICAN DIARY LITERATURE

1874   Benjamin Moran appointed minister to Portugal.

1877   Publication of the final volume of the twelve-volume diary, *Memoirs of John Quincy Adams*, edited by his son Charles Francis Adams.

1881   Mary Chesnut reworks her Civil War diary into *Diary from Dixie*.

1882   The death of Richard Henry Dana.

1886   Thomas Wentworth Higginson attends Emily Dickinson's funeral.

1889   Alice James develops her commonplace book into a true diary.

1892   Death of Alice James.

1896   John Burroughs publishes *Whitman: A Study*.

Chapter One
The Development of the American Diary

The second half of the nineteenth century begins with what has been called the "American Renaissance," a term coined to designate the time in which America was reaching its cultural "maturity."[1] That designation, which has long been questioned as it applies to a number of other literary genres, should also be questioned in regard to the diary. Diaries had been produced steadily and been an important part of American culture ever since the "great migration" that brought a wave of colonists to New England in the 1630s. A good deal of what we know about those Puritan settlers and their descendants has been preserved in diaries such as those of John Winthrop and Samuel Sewall.

Many early diaries were directed to very specific and functional objectives. For example, a large number, including those of Michael Wigglesworth and David Brainerd, were spiritual journals focusing on concerns such as the discovery of a pattern of experience that could convince the diarist that he or she had received God's grace. The Puritans were not the only group of colonial diarists to keep spiritual journals; Quakers like John Woolman and Methodists like Francis Asbury also kept them. Although the proportion of diaries that can be classed as spiritual journals has decreased, this type of diary continues to be written; and, as we shall see, it influenced the development of other types of diary literature.

Among the other diary forms important to colonial America were those prompted by travel, romance, and war. These forms too continued to be important in the nineteenth century. The late nineteenth-century diaries of Helen Carpenter and Richard Henry Dana have much in common with colonial travel diaries, such as those of Sarah Kemble Knight and Dr. Alexander Hamilton. The diary kept by Governeur Morris during his diplomatic mission to France at the time of the French Revolution is part of a tradition that includes accounts of diplomatic missions by George Mifflin Dallas and Benjamin Moran during the middle of the nineteenth century. The romance and courtship diary of Mollie Dorsey Sanford, begun in 1857, can be appreciated in the context of the works of Sally Wister and Ann Home Livingston written in the eighteenth century. Similarly, the diaries of the Revolution, such as those of James Thacher and Josiah Atkins, are related to Civil War diaries of John Beatty and Benjamin T. Smith. Union soldier John Ransom may have suffered more in Andersonville than did Charles Herbert when he was imprisoned in Britain during the Revolution, but their diaries describe similar responses to captivity.

As a group, the diaries of the nineteenth century tend to be longer and more complex than those of the seventeenth and eighteenth centuries; however, it would be a mistake to assume that the diaries of the earlier period were less expertly written. Those of Cotton Mather, John Woolman, and John Adams are of significant merit, and such complex and expertly written diaries as those of John Quincy Adams and Ralph Waldo Emerson constitute ample evidence that the diary form had achieved a high degree of sophistication prior to 1850. In writing his diary, Charles Francis Adams was very conscious that he was continuing not just his father's practice but a family tradition that could be traced back to his grandfather, John Adams. Similarly, Thoreau adopted his practice of diary keeping from the example of his spiritual father, Emerson.

The diaries written in America during the second half of the nineteenth century show that their authors had a sense that they were part of an established society. Abraham Lincoln asserted in the "Gettysburg Address," that the Civil War tested whether America would endure as a nation; however, America's survival as a culture had already been assured. Both Northerners and Southerners saw themselves as the true Americans, the rightful heirs of an American tradition stretching back into the period of colonial settlement. Both sides talked about preserving that tradition; both the South in arguing for secession and the North in advocating abolition sought to conserve rather than revolutionize. Even Southern diarists of the Civil War period, such as Andrews, Holmes, Dawson, and McGuire, were more likely to speak of the preservation of an established way of life than of the creation of a new society.

By 1850 the period of the great exploration diaries—Lewis and Clark, Pike, Schoolcraft, and Frémont—had ended. The frontier as a demarcation of the extent of settlement, the boundary between the "primitive" and the "civilized," might continue for several decades more, but the frontier as the unknown was no more. Settlements had encircled the wilderness and the surrender of the wild seemed assured. Travel diaries were still being written, but many developed into a different form, consisting primarily of a series of travel accounts. Even pioneers like Helen Carpenter traveling west in a wagon train seemed conscious that, while the experience was new for the individual, it was also a continuation of that of others.

However, the sense of so many diarists of the later nineteenth century that they were moving within an established tradition, did not mean for them as writers, and should not suggest to us as readers, that they had little new to contribute. Thomas Wentworth Higginson used his diary to remind himself, "I cannot live a past experience over again. Life is a spiral, not a circle. If I try for an instant to reproduce a past experience, except in a higher form, I shall *fail*."[2] Many of the diarists mentioned in this volume were conscious of their place in an American diary tradition, but still saw that, even when they followed the general pattern of earlier writers, they might still have the opportunity to advance their own lives as well as the diary form in which they chose to record them.

Chapter Two
Diaries of Western Travel and Settlement

Diaries related to the travel to and settlement of the West are an appropriate topic with which to begin this volume because some of them were composed before or at mid-century. Edwin Bryant's *What I Saw in California* and Walter Colton's *Three Years in California* begin in the period just before the discovery of gold in January, 1848, at Sutter's Mill. A second group of diaries written in the late 1840s and early 1850s chronicle the gold rush itself; and another diary, that of Helen McCowen Carpenter, focuses on the westward migration in the late 1850s. Other interesting travel diaries of this period are the sea-voyage diaries kept by Dr. Edward Ely and Herman Melville. And, as we shall see in later chapters, travel may play an important part in more complex diaries.

Edwin Bryant (1805–1869)

Edwin Bryant's diary was obviously revised for publication; and, as a professional journalist, he probably started his record for the purpose of eventual publication. In general, Bryant attempted to offer an account that would encourage emigration, and he included in his introduction a fanciful tale of a Californian who, kept in health by the climate, lived so long that he had tired of life. Only after leaving California was the man able to die; and, when his body was returned for burial, he was resurrected.[1] Less encouraging is a real account appended to Bryant's dairy in the form of the brief diary of an anonymous "sufferer" among the members of the Donner Party.[2]

Bryant left Independence, Missouri, shortly before word arrived there of the outbreak of war with Mexico. The diary text begins on May 5, 1846 with a flowery statement about "the beauties and glories of spring . . . unfolding themselves, and earth and sky seem[ing] to vie with each other in presenting the most pleasing influences to the

4

eye and upon the sensibilities" (19). During the early portion of the diary Bryant continued to mar his text with such overwritten prose. However, the number and extent of the more egregious instances of overwritten prose gradually decreased. Excusable exceptions include passages in which the exaggeration was intentional. One such is a humorous passage in which mosquitoes are described as having "an untiring perseverance, and a chivalry and courage equaling if not surpassing the valor of the hosts which met and fought our generals and armies in Mexico" (135).

Bryant's account is notable not only for his inclusion of descriptions containing a large measure of imaginative response, but also for his efforts in associating events with the history and legends of the frontier. A good example is the entry written as the emigrant party neared Scott's Bluff in western Nebraska. Bryant described the bluff in language that not only illustrated its physical appearance, but invested it with a mythical power: "It exhibits all the architectural shapes of arch, pillar, dome, spire, minaret, temple, gothic castle, and modern fortification . . . upon a scale [so] far surpassing the constructive efforts of human nature [that] the tower of Babel, if its builders had been permitted to proceed in their ambitious undertaking, would have been but a feeble imitation of these stupendous structures of nature." Bryant furthered his effect by providing the legend about the deserted trapper for whom the Bluffs were named (104).

In August 1846, Bryant's party finally crossed the Sierras and entered California, arriving soon at Sutter's Fort. Their arrival coincided with the beginning of the Bear Flag rebellion, and Bryant soon joined Frémont in the conquest of California. The published portion of his diary ends during this period. In February 1847, Bryant was appointed Alcalde of San Francisco by General Kearny, but he did not remain in office long and returned East in June.

Reverend Walter Colton (1797–1851)

Like Bryant, Colton also became a California official, receiving his post, Alcalde of Monterey, first as an appointment from Commodore Stockton in July 1846, and then by election in September. As Alcalde, Colton was both an administrator and judge; many of the most interesting parts of this diary describe law cases he heard. Some are humorous, such as that arising from a fight between two washerwomen when one began to wash along a section of shore that the other thought was hers: "War offensive and defensive immediately commences. One drew a knife which had a blade two mortal inches in length, and the other a sharp ivory bodkin. But what their weapons wanted in terror and strength their ungentle anger supplied." At length, Colton so settled the dispute that "Both went away declaring either margin of the pool good enough, and each urging the first choice."[3]

Colton gave a full and interesting account of California, its inhabitants, and their customs. He described courtship and marriage, the construction of ox carts and ploughs, and even the "annual egg breaking festival" in which "the natural contents of the egg . . . are blown out and the shell is filled with water, scented with cologne or lavender; or more often with gold tinsel, and flashing paper, cut into ten thousand minute particles." These eggs are then thrown at an "antagonist . . . always of the opposite sex" (143–44).

Colton was particularly impressed by the bounty of California, where "oats grow wild. The last crop plants the next, without the aid of man." And this "fecundity of nature" was not "confined to the vegetable kingdom." It was, Colton insisted, "characteristic of the animals that sport in wild life over these hills and valleys. A sheep has two lambs a year . . . and one litter of pigs follows another so fast that the squeelers and grunters are often confounded" (40). Nor was California less healthful for humans. Colton joked that it provided such an easy life that "were it possible for a man to live without the trouble of drawing his breath I should look for this pleasing phenomenon in California" (73).

Colton foresaw the effects of the American acquisition of California. Of San Francisco Bay, he wrote, "The tide of emigration is setting there with as much steadiness as the rivers roll into its capacious bosom. The day is coming when the spires of a great city will be mirrored in its waters" (61). Indeed, only a short time later Colton noted that emigrants had already begun "pouring into the rich valley of the Sacramento" and predicted that their "intelligence wealth and industry" would "change the face of California" (73).

Colton became as impressed with the people of California as with their land: "There are no people that I have ever been among who enjoy life as thoroughly as the Californians. Their habits are simple; their wants are few; nature rolls everything spontaneously into their lap"; as a result, "there is hardly a shanty among them which does not contain more true contentment, more genuine gladness of the heart than you will meet with in the most princely palace" (222–23). Colton believed that the good fortune of the Californians inspired generous natures, but he feared that they might change before the onrush of American immigration and that before too long "American avarice" would harden their hearts and make "a god of gold" (223).

Not long after this prophetic entry, Monterey "was startled out of its quiet dreams by the announcement that gold had been discovered" (242). At first the news of the gold was thought to be a rumor, but when confirmed it set off a gold fever: "The blacksmith dropped his hammer, the carpenter his plane, the mason his trowel, the farmer his sickle, the baker his loaf, the tapster his bottle. All were off to the mines" (247). Colton explained how completely the discovery of gold "upset all the social and domestic arrangements in Monterey; the master has become his own servant, and the servant his own lord" (253). Seamen deserted their ships, "forfeiting their four years' pay, and a whole platoon of soldiers from the fort [went and] left only their colors behind" (248–49). At first these changes made Colton "wish the gold mines were in the earth's flaming center, from which they sprung," but by September Colton himself had gone off to the mines (254).

The discovery of gold shifted values. Colton told of a woman who, panning for gold and finding only about a dollar and a half's worth in her bowl, "hurled it back into the water" as if "insulted by the meager amount." This event prompted him to write, "Poor woman! how little thou knowest of the patient females, who in our large cities make a shirt or vest for ten cents" (276). Colton returned from the diggings in December.

In one of his last entries Colton suggested that one of the benefits of the discovery of gold was that it would help to exclude slavery from California: "It is not that those who have come to dig gold care about slavery or its abolition, but that rather that those who would seek gold knew that "they must dig themselves . . . and they won't degrade their calling by associating it with slave labor." Colton maintained that slavery debased the value of all labor and that, given their pride in their accomplishments, the Californian emigrants would insist on their "right to shape and settle things their own way" (374).

Daniel B. Woods (dates unknown)

Numerous diaries were begun in response to and devoted to the California gold rush.[4] Among the best of these as a literary work is Daniel B. Woods's *Sixteen Months at the Gold Diggings.* With the exception of those diaries heavily rewritten for publication, Woods's diary is among the most thematically unified.

While the search for gold is the subject of the diary, Woods does not suggest that others follow him to California; rather he stresses that the difficulties of seeking gold often outweigh any benefits. In his preface Woods admits that one motive in publishing the diary is to "induce all who are doing *well enough* . . . to remain satisfied at home."[5] He admits that some men had made thousands in a few days, but also that others fared poorly. His entries include one account of the suffering of one young man who had died while working alone so that "not even his name could be discovered," and of another, a man of seventy, who had "left a wife and seven children at home" to seek wealth, but who, though "industrious," could not make "enough to buy his provisions" (63). Woods shows that "no kind of work is so uncertain. A miner may happen upon a good location in his very first attempt, and in a very few days make his hundreds or thousands, while the old miners about him may do nothing" (56–57).

Woods presents tantalizing examples of the success that made so many miners persist in their labors, although they themselves gained little. Like the losers at a slot machine, they needed only to see an occasional winner to convince themselves that one more attempt might bring them a fortune. Even if most miners gained little gold, they still believed that "pounds of pure virgin gold lying in lumps and scales . . . [might be] awaiting their slightest effort to transfer it to their own pockets" because they would see or hear of experiences such as the following: "The lump of gold found at Sonora . . . weighs . . . twenty-two pounds. The miner through whom I received my information had a claim next to the one in which this lump was found. It lay within two inches of the very spot where he was at work. One blow of the pick would have given him possession of it" (111). Stories of great finds were common in the camps, and each new tale might lead its hearers to a fortune or a wild goose chase.

November 9, 1850, was Woods's "last day at the mines." His decision to give up seems to have been prompted by sickness which swept his mining camp, but his efforts as a miner followed upon a particularly discouraging event. He and his associates had been searching for a vein of gold, "led on by the hope of reaching one of those rare deposits in which thousands are found." They had heard of just such a strike in their neighborhood and thought "Why might we not strike it also?" However, just as the signs seemed favorable, the dam that he and his friends had built collapsed, flooding their mining site (164–65). As he left the next day he looked back at the camp with mixed emotions. There stood "scenes of disappointment and sadness—of broken hopes and broken hearts," the wreckage of his "aqueduct and canal" and the "graves of . . . lost companions"; but there too were the places where he and his companions had met to organize their company and pray to God; there too was his own dwelling with its "last fire still smoking" (165–66). On November 26, he set sail for New York.

Helen McCowen Carpenter (1838–1917)

Women in this period faced limitations on their educations, roles, and opportunities for expression; yet many produced fine diaries. The private nature of the diary form often provided them with a means to deal with subjects and express attitudes not sanctioned by the male-dominated society in which they lived. Moreover, some women diarists were in positions to produce particularly valuable records. This situation is especially evident in their diaries of the westward migration.

Women's diaries have increasingly become an important source for studies about women, and several of these studies have led to the discovery and publication of diaries of literary merit. Among these studies are Lillian Schlissel's *Women's Diaries of the Westward Journey* and Elizabeth Hampsten's *Read This Only to Yourself: The Private Diaries of Midwestern Women, 1880–1910*. While they focus on the historical and sociological value that comes from examining westward emigration and frontier settlement from a woman's point of view, these studies also demonstrate the literary quality of many of the diaries they consider. One of the best women's diaries of the frontier is that of Helen McCowen Carpenter.

Carpenter's diary of "A Trip Across the Plains in an Ox Wagon, 1857" begins "Ho—for California—at last we are on the way—only seven miles from home (which is to be home no longer) yet we have really started, and with good luck may some day reach the 'promised land.'"[6] Married just four months when her diary began on May 26, Carpenter considered the journey to California as her "bridal trip" (95). In this context all experience had a double novelty and the trip's symbolic meaning as a passage between two phases in her life is emphasized.

Early in the diary Carpenter reflects on leaving Kansas, where she had lived for the previous two years; this material helps to provide insights into her character and convictions. In one entry she explains wryly that, despite such *"allurements"* as "the violent thunderstorms [which] are enough to wreck the nerves of Hercules and the rattle-snakes . . . as thick as the leaves on the trees," she could "bid Kansas Good Bye with out a regret" and with some pride for her part in making it a "free state" (96).

Carpenter's initial reaction to the journey was positive. She found beauty in the way the camp looked: "The five wagons with white drilling covers (double thickness over the top) are looking much dressed up as they stand in a semicircle in the waving green grass. The cattle and horses, 100 or more in all, are off to one side grazing and the camp fires within the circle are burning brightly inviting the cooks to get to work" (94). This excellent description allows the reader to experience and to understand the way of life of these pioneers. It is a good example of Carpenter's skill as a diarist.

Carpenter's use of details is particularly valuable; in describing items, she emphasized the particular features that made them notable, for example: "Our wagon has square bows, which makes it much more roomy than the rounded bows. Inside the cover on each side are pockets in which odds and ends may be stowed. . . . a spring seat painted bright red sits bolt upright in the front and refuses to budge, regardless of size or weight so we are not relying on this for much in the way of comfort." She even made meaningful for readers what seems, at first, a dry list of about a dozen items that constituted her cooking equipment by the addition of a statement that she was not concerned about having so little to cook with because "what we are to have to eat is going to be of much more importance than how it is cooked or served" (95).

Carpenter also gives the reader a sense of the relationships between the characters she encountered and the way the members of the wagon functioned as a society. She was astute enough to recognize that even the absence of social interaction might be considered important. After one incident, which Carpenter feared might make a reader think that her family was not "sociable or on good terms with our fellow travelers," she explained:

The plain fact of the matter is we have no time for sociability. From the time we get up in the morning until we are on the road it is hurry-scurry to get breakfast and put away the things that necessarily had to be pulled out last night. While under way there is no room in the wagon for a visitor. Nooning

is barely long enough to get a cold bite and at night. . . . although there is
not much to cook, the difficulty and inconvenience in doing it amounts to a
good deal. So that by the time one has squatted about the fire and cooked
bread and bacon, made several trips to and from the wagon, washed the dishes
(with no place to drain them), and gotten things ready for an early breakfast,
some of the others already have their night caps on. (114)

This passage offers an excellent example of the way Carpenter weaves
a group of details from the everyday activities of a pioneer woman into
a unified narrative.

Her entries range from harsh tales of illness and death to lighter
episodes about a young man's fiddling. Some of these experiences,
which seem self-contained episodes, later prove to be related, forming
one of the subplots of the diary. One such subplot involves the Carpenters' encounter with Mr. Dobbins. Despite misgivings on the part
of Mrs. Carpenter and her mother about Dobbins's "manner," especially his mistreatment of some young men in his party, the Carpenter
men decided to travel with him because of his superior knowledge of
the trail (140–41). The Carpenters soon became concerned about the
slow pace at which Dobbins had them travel because it made them fall
well behind all the other wagon trains and so become more vulnerable
to Indian attack. However, the men accepted his contention that his
pace would keep the teams in better condition.

Carpenter's husband and her father finally came to doubt Dobbins
during an Indian raid on the livestock. Carpenter told how the "bullets
came whizzing through camp" and insisted that "none can know the
horror of this who has not been similarly situated." After the stock was
safe, the party noticed that "Dobbins was not with the others. Where
was Dobbins? He was found just as far back in one of his wagons as he
could get and there he sat with two guns." His excuse for this cowardice was that he thought "it was not safe to go and leave the women and
children alone." However, as Carpenter told her diary, "they were as
safe without him as with him" (154–56).

Finally, the Carpenters decided to "rush ahead" so that they could
overtake the larger wagon trains ahead. Given Dobbins's cowardice,
they were surprised when he still chose to stay back. Later this mystery
was resolved: Dobbins had been collecting stray cattle from the trains
ahead. As Carpenter explains, "His greed is still greater than his cowardice which we thought could not be excelled. For the sake of those
few cattle, all our lives were risked" (170).

In the last month of the journey the Carpenters' cattle and oxen began to die from lack of food and water and from the "hard travel" (179). On October 22 the experience ended happily: "we are quite happy in the thought that all of our earthly belongings are no longer to be packed in an old ox wagon each morning and set treking westward" (188).

Chapter Three
War Diaries I—Military

No event during the nineteenth century so dislocated the normal pattern of life in America as did the Civil War; and, therefore, it should not seem surprising that the war prompted the creation of a large number of diaries. The number and quality of these overshadow those written in response to all of the other American military conflicts during the century. Of course, the same pressures of war that prompted so many of these military diaries also served as an impediment to their success as literary works. While many of those kept by soldiers contain significant historical information, and some have sections that have the full entries necessary for a well-written account, few merit attention as literature. Just as with the soldiers of the Revolution, few active soldiers in the Civil War were able to devote the time necessary to keep diaries of the quality we have been considering. As the Confederate soldiers often had to combat a larger and better-supplied opposition, they had less time to devote to art than those of the Union, a situation which may explain why the diaries covered in this chapter are by Northerners. And it is probably not a coincidence that these diaries were written by an officer, an officer's orderly, a prisoner, and some government officials, persons whose roles freed them from some of the demands on ordinary soldiers.

John Beatty (1828–1914)

John Beatty, a staunch Republican and a member of the electoral college that chose Lincoln in 1860, was among the early Union volunteers. On June 22, 1861, as Beatty was about to enter what is now West Virginia, he began a diary that he continued until about a month before his resignation from military service.

There was little fighting in the period covered by the first part of the diary. Beatty wrote that while he had heard "rumors of skirmishes and small fights a few miles off . . . as yet the only gunpowder we have smelled is our own."[1] It is doubtful that he regretted this lack of action, for while the literary side of his mind (Beatty would later publish three novels and historical articles) was often engaged by the monumental nature of the war, its scenes, and its impact, he did not relish the death and danger that came with it. "Our boys," he wrote, "look forward . . . to a day of battle as one of rare sport. I do not. I endeavor to picture to myself all of its terrors, so that I may not be surprised and dumfounded when the shock comes. Our army is probably now making one of the most interesting chapters of American history. God grant it may be a chapter our northern people will not be ashamed to read" (24). This sense, not only of the historical, but also of the literary aspect of the war that would become the subject matter for the diary is a controlling element of the work.

Beatty proved unusually accurate in his early predictions of the war. Although before the battle of Bull Run most Northerners expected a quick victory, Beatty realized that the Southerners, having been "made to believe that they . . . [were] in the right" and that the Northerners were "invaders come to conquer and destroy," would make the war a long and costly one. He also predicted that, although the war was not initially a "war of emancipation," it would end slavery in America. Beatty favored such a development and wished from the beginning that he might "commence the work of emancipation at once and leave every foot of soil behind me free" (24).

Beatty was willing to display courage when he thought it necessary, but he saw no purpose in needless risk. In one instance he was ordered by a pompous superior to engage in a reconnaissance that he considered a "fool's errand." Feeling that his attempts to question the scheme had called his courage into question and "determined to risk the lives of no others," Beatty set out alone to ride "half a mile behind the enemy's outposts" (25). On another occasion, his men seemed afraid to advance as ordered, and Beatty sought to set an example. Riding forward, he found "I have done a foolish thing. A hundred muskets open on me from the woods; but the eyes of my own brigade and of other troops are on me and I cannot back out . . . the bullets whistle like bees about my head, but I ride the whole length of the proposed skirmish line and get back to the brigade in safety" (158).

Even in the midst of such dangers Beatty expressed a poetic (albeit a highly romanticized) interest in the scenery. Standing outside his tent one summer morning gazing at a mountain peak, "now in sunshine, then in shadow, and the light and sunshine chasing each other from point to point over the mountains," Beatty came to feel that "God, as at Sinai, has set his foot upon the earth." Moving from this divine "panorama" to speculations on the relationship between man and his environment, the diarist wrote:

I can almost believe now that men become, to some extent, like the country in which they live. In the plain country the inhabitants learn to traffic, come to regard money-getting as the great object in life, and have but a dim perception of those higher emotions from which spring the noblest acts. In a mountain country God has made many things sublime, and some things very beautiful. . . . Like the country may we not look to find the people unpolished, rugged and uneven, capable of the noblest heroism or the most infernal villainy—their lives full of lights and shadows, elevations and depressions? (33–34)

Beatty was quick to see that not only was this "dense wilderness" a fit "country for the romancer," a setting for "plumed knights" and "imaginary Robin Hoods," but also that the battlefields on which he had fought and the war over which "neighbors have divided and families separated" offered the poet everything "but the invention to construct the plot of his tale and the genius to breathe life into the characters." He foresaw that after the passage of time, "truth, courage and honesty will finally triumph. . . . the blue and the gray will meet to fight and be reconciled" on the pages of novels (266–67).

The war provided Beatty with scenery befitting a novel and with a wealth of characters comparable to those he had seen in fiction. The "fighting parson" of an Indiana regiment standing at the scene of a battle with "two revolvers and a hatchet in his belt appeared more like a firebrand of war than a minister of peace" and reminded the diarist of "Scott's Holy Clerk of Copamhurst, or the fighting friar of the times of Robin Hood." The captain, who in tales of "hairbreadth escapes" portrayed himself as "the most formidable man alive," recalled for Beatty Shakespeare's "Ancient Pistol come again to astonish the world by deeds of reckless daring" (42–43).

A large number of these portraits are humorous, if not intensely satirical. In one entry Beatty told of a superstitious colonel who believed in dreams and did not like "to see the moon through brush," but who behaved with bravery in battle because he was convinced "that his time to die had not yet come" (120–21).

In his anecdotes Beatty's ear for dialogue helped him to capture the

flavor of an incident, such as a "debate" with a black known in camp
as Old Tom who argued that white skin was a mark of original
sin:

"Pears to me . . . hab to tell de truf, sah; dat's my min'. Men was 'riginally
black; but de Lord he scar him till he got white; dat's de reasonable supposi-
tion, sah. Do a man's har git black when he's scared sah? No, sah, it gits
white. Did you ebber know a man ter get black when he's scared, sah? No,
sah, he gits white."
"That does seem to be a knock-down argument, Tom."
"Yes, sah, I've argied with mor'n a hunded white men sah, an' they can
never git aroun dat pint." (235–36)

Unlike the characters in a novel, however, most of those in Beatty's
diary make only brief appearances. The only sustained portrait is that
of Beatty himself, who was capable of poking the same kind of fun at
himself that he directed at others. For example, when he was promoted
to brigadier general, he suggested that in his case B.G. would "probably stand for big goose" (186). However, he also had a stubborn pride,
a strong temper, and a tendency to impulsiveness that often got him
into trouble. Punishing a drunken soldier who had been "saucy and
insubordinate," Beatty personally tied the man to a tree, an action that
stirred the hatred of the regiment. But though given to such bursts of
temper, Beatty usually admitted his faults. In this case he realized,
although almost too late, that he had committed "a high-handed out-
rage upon the person of a volunteer soldier, the last and worst of the
many arbitrary and severe acts of which I had been guilty" (74–75).
    In the Civil War only a small portion of a soldier's time was spent
in actual combat, and readers should not be surprised that most of
Beatty's diary deals with incidents in camp. He handles such material
exceptionally well; his strategies for presenting life in camp have surprising variety and originality. For example, one series of entries shows
different characters and activities through the songs being sung: the
cat-like wails of a "happy party . . . are exercising their lungs on a
negro melody" about "de kingdom comin' / And de year of jubelo"
(171), happy "Irish melodies" saluting "Dear Erin . . . An emerald set
in the ring of the sea" (173), the cook's "devotional refrain . . . 'I'm
guien home, / To d-i-e no mo'" (177), and a "warble" in broken English "und such ding I never did see in my life" (179). These strains
are presented intermixed with "the faintest possible sound of a violin"

(179), shouts of "Vive l'America" (178), and the "humming [of] a ditty about true love" (175).

Although only a portion of the diary describes actual fighting, there are full and well-rendered accounts of battles, including major engagements at Murfreesboro, Chickamauga, and Missionary Ridge. Beatty tells of having his horse shot from under him and of a soldier walking beside him being "struck between the shoulders by a ricocheting ball and instantly killed" (156).

Beatty uses a variety of devices effectively to heighten the battle scenes. One of the most prominent is the shift from the past tense used in most of the diary to the present. This shift sometimes produced an uncharacteristically staccato style, and gives such entries a sense of immediacy:

As we start, the battery commences to shell the woods. As we get nearer the objective point, I put the men on the double-quick. The rebels, discovering our approach, open a heavy fire, but in the darkness shoot too high. The blaze of their guns reveals their exact position to us. We reach the rude log breastworks behind which they are standing and grapple with them. Colonel Humphrey receives a severe thrust from a bayonet; others are wounded and some are killed. It is pitch dark under the trees. (158)

Beatty's imagery also contributes to the diary. He pictures the cannon shot rolling up the road "like balls on a bowling alley" (156), and personifies two batteries as "gigantic gentlemen" who "got into an angry discussion" (259–60). Indeed the Union artillery seemed a "national giant [which] appeared to skip from point to point . . . as if seeking a weak place in his antagonist's armor" (263).

At the end of the diary Beatty looks back at these battles and prophesies that some day historians will record "the thrilling tragedies enacted" there, poets illuminate "every hilltop and mountain peak," and novelists people them from their imaginations (272). He tried not only to give an accurate account of the real events but also to begin the shift into such mythologizing. One cannot be certain that, as Harvey S. Ford, Beatty's most recent editor, implies in his preface, Beatty's complaints in some of his last entries about the dullness of camp life help to explain his decision to resign from the army and end his military diary. It seems more likely that Beatty recognized that he had achieved his objectives as solider and diarist. In January 1864, it may not have been obvious to everyone that the turning point of the war had been reached, but Beatty seems to have been sufficiently attuned to the trends to have seen its inevitable end.

Benjamin T. Smith (1844–1908)

Benjamin Smith was only seventeen when he decided to enter the Union army as an infantry private. The diary begins on October 8, 1861, the day of his enlistment (an introductory entry seems sufficiently different in style from the next entries to suggest it may have been added later). Smith was in many of the same campaigns as Beatty and shares Beatty's tendencies toward romanticized descriptions; however, these diaries have markedly different flavors. Although Beatty attempted to insert some humor in his work, and Smith more than occasionally lapsed into flowery passages,[2] the reader will be quick to discern Smith's light, relaxed manner from Beatty's self-consciously dramatic one. Smith seems especially resilient and characteristically determined to adapt to new situations. For example, when he has to sleep on a pair of rails suspended over some marshy ground in such a way that "the least movement to either side would tumble . . . [him] into the mud," he concludes that "one may do most any thing by trying hard enough" (30).

Even when Smith receives what he calls "the saddest news," he submerges it in an entry about a muddy road: "It has been raining with great regularity, mud is the predominant feature of the landscape, never the less we are tramping along towards Corinth Miss. The road is just horrible, mud puddles, and mud without puddles" (35). Only when he has reached the appropriate place in chronological sequence does he write of receiving news of his mother's death. He briefly tells of brooding and regretting the loss of the opportunity to repay her for her kindnesses, but soon switches back to talk about sleeping on the wet ground and the way "the sharp crack of the thunder sounded like the distant charge of artillery, while the almost constant play of the lightning looked like the flashes of a thousand guns" (37). The passage as a whole can be taken as a repressed comment on the general destructive power of nature, a power that Smith usually accepts with resignation or humor.

This humor is apparent from Smith's first lines in which he explains that work in the "scorching" summer fields has not been "altogether congenial." Without a direct statement he lets the reader know that he is dissatisfied with the prospect of serving as the inadequate assistant to his older brothers. His subsequent decision to go to the county seat and "see if they have any use for a boy of seventeen" in the army seems to have been more than just a "boyish" reaction to news of the first Union defeats (4–5). At the very least it seems influenced by his relationship with his brothers, who laughed at his proposed enlistment. This impression is reinforced in a subsequent entry; there is a sense of pride in Smith's description of the moment his company paraded past his house: "I looked neither to the right or left but from the corner of my eye, I see Joe and Jonas [his brothers] watching us file by" (10).

In the months that followed, Smith and his company were at the scenes of major battles, including Shiloh, but they were only at the edge of things. Then on May 28, 1862, he experienced battle:

The gunners lay down with the lanyards in hand, and awaited the expected charge of the enemy. Nor had we long to wait, for soon the woods was filled with their yells as they came. . . . On they came in swift advance, yelling like bedlamites let loose; when they had reached a proper distance, up rose the gunners and fired death and destruction into their ranks. At point blank range wide swaths were cut through the rebel ranks; they staggered and stopped. Another discharge followed and the enemy turned and ran for dear life. (42)

About a year after his enlistment Smith had become a corporal in a "company of mounted scouts" (50). Soon he was trained in "riding in all gates, jumping logs and ditches, firing [from horseback and] . . . charging with sabers drawn" (54). Then, in May, 1863, Smith became an escort and orderly to General Sheridan. In this capacity he had the opportunity to get a different perspective on the fighting and the time to write about his impressions. In this period he was at the scene of a number of major engagements, including the battle of Chattanooga.

Nature and the tensions of war sometimes inspired Smith to record romantic musings, as at Lookout Mountain, where he rhapsodized over the sun's "rays penetrating far beneath a lake" of unknown depth, "The surface still as death" forming "a wild scene" he would "not soon forget" (88–89). Similarly, in an entry written in anticipation of battle, an anxious Smith was inspired by the "cold and frosty" night. Lying in the dark, he looked up at the sky, and its beauty awakened a melodramatic strain. The "bright stars" and "the round silver moon, resting at peace up there in the blue vault of Heaven" brought thoughts of "the upturned cold white faces of the hundreds of the dead, motionless as they lay all over the field; they are at peace. At the roll of the drum, in the morning, calling to arms again, to renew the strife, they will not respond, but sleep peacefully on through the deadly strife to follow" (91–92).

Although Smith's position in the general's staff kept him away from many of the dangers of battle, he could never be completely secure. In one encounter he had seemed relatively safe as part of the escort for the commanding generals, but, stopping to take a drink at a spring, Smith suddenly found himself cut off as the army unexpectedly pulled back. He wrote in his diary, "the bullets flew around me, one passing through my hair on the back of my neck" (99). Having no provisions with him, Smith took a pack from a dead soldier: "The poor fellow back there on the field, of death, dreamed not that he was providing for a comrade when he filled his sack." Finally, "guided by the sounds of battle," Smith made his way back to the safety of the Union lines (101).

As the following excerpt illustrates, Smith's descriptions of battle began to be written in poetic cadences with an obvious use of alliteration and a rhythmic pattern that is so regular it almost tempts the reader to break the passage into lines:

Ceaseless has the battle raged all day long; charges and repulses, with countercharges by the enemy, which were repulsed at each endeavor; encounters between the works in open field each side charging the other in desperate action. (192)

Even when Smith seems to have become most accustomed to war, or when his descriptions of battle assumed a "poetic" tone, the destruction of war never really became usual or beautiful. The reader is never allowed to move too far from an awareness that "Men have been slaughtered . . . or disabled" (192). If Smith wrote of heroism, he matched it with scenes of suffering such as the following, reminiscent of sections of Whitman's *Leaves of Grass*:

The ambulance corps are busily engaged in searching for the wounded, whether friend or foe. They are taken up, and conveyed to the surgeons tents; here they are laid upon a table and examined, bullets are probed for, wounds stitched up and dressed, arms and legs cut off if too badly shattered to be saved. Indiscriminately, blue or gray, are attended to. . . . [In one tent I find the surgeon] with his assistants, up to their elbows in gore; in one corner is a pile of members of the human system, arms and legs, hands and feet. A confederate is stretched on a table . . . with a sponge held to his nose; he is unconscious that his right limb is being sawed off just below the knee. (192–93)

The diary is marked by descriptions of scenes and events beyond the actual fighting. During a battle Smith shows us a general deep in thought:

Genl. Thomas . . . is sitting upon the end of a log, his right elbow resting on his knee, with his hand nursing his stubby whiskers. He is alone, his staff standing by their horses within call in a slight depression below him, the bullets are kicking up the dust all around his vicinity; they seem not to be a disturbing element to his motionless figure.

It may be a fateful day with him, for today will decide for him; in success his promotion, in defeat, he is undone. The hissing of the bullets, nor the screech of the passing shells disturb him not; he is as motionless as the log upon which he sits. (195)

In these few lines Smith captures the soul of a moment with a few sure strokes. The sense of immobility makes the passage seem like a painting, with the general in the center, his posture directing the viewer's eye outward toward the commotion of battle, while the gaze of his attendants and track of bullet and shell return the focus to the still center.

Smith's record gives the reader a feel for a soldier's life: the cooks bringing up "great pails of steaming hot coffee, and cooked meat" after a battle (192), the execution of bounty jumpers, or the stubborn behavior of an army mule. He also includes descriptions of sightseeing, visits, dances and theater performances during furloughs and briefer periods of calm. Smith also offers numerous skillfully written humorous anecdotes, such as the story of a rebel captain who when captured protested, "'I would rather be shot than surrender, a disgrace I can not tolerate' [until a Union soldier] . . . said, as he placed the cold muzzle of a revolver in his face, 'All right Captain, I will save your honor'" (159).

On April 8, 1865, Smith, on furlough in Chicago, received news of the fall of Richmond. While "general rejoicing is the order of the day," he writes of being saddened by memories of all the men "that sacrificed their lives for freedom's cause, whose bones now lie buried in the far off south, on the battlefield and plain with scarce a mound to mark the spot where they fell" (210). The diarist had become a very different man from the boy who had gone away to war thinking of childhood battle royals with "clods and turfs" (6).

Any joy Smith might have felt at the prospect of the war's end was further reduced by news of Lincoln's death. He was one of those thousands in Chicago who, on May 1, 1865, viewed the body of the late president lying in state: "As I gaze upon the homely features, so still and motionless, homely in life, beautiful in death, I think of the old honest Abe whom the soldiers loved so well" (215–16).

A few days later Smith returned to his post, but the war was over. In November he made application to be mustered out of the service. On the fifth he was in Springfield, Illinois, visiting Lincoln's grave, and two days later he was "a soldier no more." It seems significant that his comments written on that day include the words, "I turn my back upon the past" (231). He was only twenty-one. The diary, although too important to be discarded, was, as a part of the past, something to be left behind with the war. On November 8 he penned his final entry:

. . . and for the last time I will scribble a line or two in my faithful journal, and then bid you farewell. You have been my constant companion for four years. I have guarded you as the apple of my eye, not knowing whether you would someday be finished completely or if perchance your career might be brought to a sudden end through the mishaps of war. My one constant companion through out the struggle, in the peaceful camp, or the silent picket line, tramping on foot or in the saddle. . . . On the field of battle when the bullets flew too thick for comfort or the screeching shell burst and scattered the fragments around us you were there too. . . . Holding between your covers, a true history of passing events, if in future years I turn to your pages, seeking to refresh my memory, I will know your record is reliable. (231–32)

The entry almost seems a psalm, a prayer, to a protecting God. The dangers that prompted Smith's regular devotions were over, but not some deeper faith that might be called upon in the future.

John L. Ransom (1843–18??)

Although published under the title *Andersonville Diary*, only about one third of the diary deals with Ransom's experiences there.[3] The balance includes periods in which he was in several other prisons and prison hospitals or involved in escapes. But the diary has been aptly titled, for, eventually, almost everything in it came to be considered in its relation to the period in Andersonville. Even the long initial section dealing with his imprisonments at Belle Isle near Richmond and the Pemberton Building in Richmond eventually became subordinated to the diarist's experiences at Andersonville either through later comparisons or, as in the following excerpt, through denial of the possibility of comparison:

> Wish I had the gift of description, that I might describe this place. . . . Thought Belle Isle was a very bad place and used about the worst language I knew how to use in describing it, and so find myself at fault in depicting matters here as they are. At Belle Isle we had good water and plenty of it, and I believe it depends more upon water than food as regards to health. We also had good pure water from up the James River. Here we have the very worst kind of water. Nothing can be nastier than the stream drizzling its way through the camp. And as for air to breathe, it is what arises from this foul place. On all four sides of us are high walls and tall trees, and there is apparently no wind to blow away the stench, and we are obliged to breathe and live in it. Dead bodies lay around all day in the broiling sun, by the dozens, even hundreds, and we must suffer and live in this horrible atmosphere. It is too horrible for me to describe in fitting language. . . . It's too stupendous an undertaking. *Only those who are here will ever know what Andersonville is.* (113–14)

Ransom did a far better job of describing the horrors of Andersonville than this passage suggests. Even those readers who are not particularly squeamish would not want a more vivid description of the suffering than, "To-day saw a man with a bullet hole in his head over an inch deep, and you could look down in it and see maggots squirming around at the bottom" (92).

Early in his imprisonment Ransom could be frightened by the sight of some "old prisoners, nearly naked, very dirty and poor, some of them sick, lying on the cold ground with nothing under them or over them, and no fire . . . the very picture of despair with hollow eyes, sunken cheeks and haggard expression" (37), but it took only a little time in Andersonville before "some of the most horrible sights that can possibly be" had become "common every day occurrences" (100), and even the most terrifying sights and conditions prompted only a restrained response (93). In describing the dead and dying, Ransom makes comparisons that show the dehumanization of the prisoners: "They die like sheep fully a hundred each day" (99); "they go like a horse that will stand up until he drops dead," and then the body along with twenty or thirty more, "just like four foot wood is loaded on to a wagon" to be carted off to the graveyard (100). Ransom came to expect this end as his own. Teeth loose from scurvy, "legs swollen up with dropsy," he believed himself "on the road to the trenches" prepared for the dead (93). Indeed, at one point Ransom fainted and awoke to find himself piled with the dead (126).

Such horrors are closer to those in accounts from twentieth-century concentration camps than to those in earlier American captivity diaries such as Charles Herbert's.[4] In one entry Ransom wrote, "I have read in my earlier years about prisoners in the revolutionary war and other wars. It sounded noble and heroic to be a prisoner of war, and accounts of their adventures were quite romantic; but the romance has been knocked out of the prisoner of war business, higher than a kite" (97–98).

There was a real heroism in the camps, but it was a far different sort than that in the romantic accounts Ransom refers to. In one entry we learn that one Union sergeant in the camp was really a lieutenant who, when his company was captured, "preferred to go with them and share their trials, than go with the officers" (33). At another time one of Ransom's friends risked punishment to steal supplies from a storehouse and to distribute them to his fellow prisoners (35). The diary shows that such unselfish behavior had its rewards in providing a sustaining motivation. Some prisoners so despaired that they went crazy or suicidally crossed the "dead line" where they knew they would be shot by rebel guards (94).

The diary reveals that the initial period of captivity was often crucial in determining whether or not a prisoner would turn toward such a self-destructive course. Ransom initially had such a tendency, as he reveals in the first entry, reporting his attempt to ignore George Hendryx, who had been "one of the most valued friends I had in the regiment, this action [Ransom admitted] . . . will seem strange, as indeed it is. Did not want to see him or anyone else I had seen before" (13). But Hendryx proved a true friend and soon arranged for Ransom to join a group banding together for survival. The importance of such cooperation is observable in little things as well as major ones. For example, the wood distributed to each man was too little to be of use, but "two or three can put their wood together and boil a little coffee made from bread crusts" (15).

Ransom's group, which humorously styled itself the "Astor House Mess," established regulations for their better survival: "Must take plenty of exercise, keep clean, free as circumstances will permit of vermin, drink no water until it has been boiled, which process purifies it and makes it more healthy, are not allowed to let ourselves to get despondent, and must talk laugh and make light of our affairs as possible. Sure death for a person to give up and lose all ambition" (18). The diarist quickly realized that "very many who now die, would have lived if they adopted the rules that our mess has, and lived up to them" (34).

Laughter was useful in keeping up the spirits of the prisoners, as a number of humorous entries suggest. Ransom, writing that Hendryx and he were so "attached to one another" that he didn't "believe that either one would steal from the other," added, "I certainly wouldn't take anything short of pumpkin pie or something of that sort. Of course a man would steal pie, at least we all say so, and Lewis declares he would steal dough cakes and pancakes such as his wife used to make" (52).

Like Herbert, Ransom and some of his friends were enterprising, especially a Minnesota Indian named Battese who seems to have been constantly at work. Ransom explains how, with instruction from Battese, he made a washboard and sign to earn extra food (84–85). Business became so good that he could joke about setting up an organization complete with titles for his "company" and asserted that if he and his companions could get a razor to open a barbershop, their "fortunes would be made." However, the underlying seriousness of the prisoners' predicament is never absent from the diary for long, and later in the entry Ransom adds that by this enterprise he and his fellows were able to trade for such "luxuries" as "a little real meat soup with a piece of onion in it" to prolong the life of one of their group (84–85). These mutual efforts went beyond the acquisition of such "luxuries"; at times they were essential for survival. Indeed, at one point, Battese, who came to care for Ransom "like a father" (125), saved the diarist's life by helping him to get out of Andersonville. Battese was also responsible for saving the diary, keeping two of the books when Ransom was too sick to care for anything (147).

Unfortunately, Andersonville did not always bring out men's instinct for cooperation. As Ransom recognized, "A man shows exactly what he is in Andersonville. No occasion to be any different from what you really are. Very often you see a great big fellow in size, in reality a baby in action, actually sniveling and crying, and then again you will see some runt, 'not bigger than a pint of cider,' tell the big fellow to 'brace up' and be a man. . . . there are noble big fellows as well as noble little ones" (121–22). While for some prisoners suffering inspired "noble" cooperation, others seized the opportunity to prey on their fellows, making "a ration of bread . . . often of more consequence than a man's life" (19). One group of prisoners became "cut-throats, who do nearly as they please, cheating, robbing," beating, and even killing their fellow prisoners (31). These "raiders" preyed especially on new prisoners, who often came with money and good clothing.

Banding together, the members of the "Astor House Mess" remained relatively safe from the raiders, but they knew their time would come. Several attempts to combat the raiders failed, but finally the prisoners formed a police force, captured the raiders, and with the permission of the Confederate jailers hanged six of the ringleaders. Ransom's long account of the hanging treats the incident from several angles. He examines the speeches by the condemned, the reactions of the crowd, and even a symbolic parallel suggested by the speech of Captain Wirtz, the Confederate commander of the prison (later executed as a war criminal), who made a Pilate-like declaration that, as the raiders had been tried by the Union prisoners, he "washed his hands of the whole matter." Ransom even tells how the scaffold and ropes were "carried off" by the prisoners to be used as fuel or kept as "momentoes" (114–18). However, while the putting down of the raiders brought some relief, the ultimate effect was minor. The next day Ransom wrote: "Good order has prevailed since the hanging. The men settled right down to the business of dying, with no interruption" (119).

The controlling source of tension in the diary is, very obviously, imprisonment, the diary beginning sixteen days after Ransom's capture on November 6, 1863, and ending on Christmas, 1864, two days after his safe return to Union territory. Ransom soon became aware of the diary's importance. In one early entry he wrote: "we were all searched again to-day, but I still keep my diary, although expecting to lose it every day; would be quite a loss, as the longer I write and remain a prisoner the more I am attached to the record of passing events" (49). Sometimes Ransom said that he was writing the diary only for himself, while at others he admitted that he had some expectation of publication (perhaps prompted by the earlier captivity accounts he mentioned having read). During his final escape he wrote: "Shall print this diary, and make my everlasting fortune, and when wealthy will visit this country and make every negro who has helped us millionaires" (207). But the true value of the diary could not be measured in dollars. The diary was important to Ransom's survival. When in looking over the diary he found it "nothing but grumblings and growlings," he realized that he "had best enumerate some of the better things of this life," for without hope he would soon die (101). And even when death seemed inescapable, his confidence that the diary would survive even if he didn't offered him some sense of immortality (132).

Ransom's period of diary keeping and imprisonment was paralleled by his possession of a blanket roll that by warding off the cold in winter and sun in summer repeatedly saved his life. This blanket, which he acquired shortly after his capture and lost just before he reached safety, was more than a physical aid. It seems to have almost mystical properties as the symbol of Ransom's spirit and his will to survive. When he recuperated in a hospital after getting out of Andersonville, his "old coverlid was washed and fumigated" in a parallel recovery (139). Parting from a companion who had proved untrustworthy, he writes, "am again alone and walking about the prison with my coverlid on my shoulders. Am determined that this covering protects none but thoroughly good and square fellows" (172), and when he made his final escape it was in the company of two cousins who "have also each a good blanket" (191). The coverlid, which was physically a protection against the elements, came to symbolize a general protection against all destructive forces, including the raiders, who would have stolen it, and the unworthy acquaintances, who would have debased it.

Gideon Welles (1802–1878)

After a long autobiographical section, Welles's true diary begins in August 1862, a time of great challenge to the Union. As secretary of the Navy, Welles was particularly concerned about the threat of the Confederate ironclads and the difficulty that the Union forces were having in capturing Vicksburg. The diary ends in May 1869, shortly after Welles left the government.

The facts that Welles was not a soldier, and that over half of his diary was written after the end of the Civil War make the placement of the diary in a chapter on military diaries subject to question. Yet Welles was not simply an observer of the war; he was an active participant, and his diary of the Reconstruction period was related to the war.

Though the bulk of the diary seems a history of the war as waged and perceived by the government in Washington, Welles made little attempt to disguise his personal feeling under the cover of objective history. This personalization can be illustrated by comparing his entry dealing with a cabinet meeting held on September 2, 1862, with an account of the same event in the diary of Salmon Chase, the Secretary of the Treasury. Chase wrote:

All agreed that we needed a change in Commander of the Army. . . . Mr. Welles was of the same judgment, though less positive in expression. . . . The Secretary of War [Stanton] came in. In answer to some inquiry, the fact was stated, by the President or the Secretary, that [General] McClellan had been placed in command of the forces to defend the Capital. . . . I remarked that this could be done equally well by the Engineer who constructed the Forts and that putting McClellan in command for this purpose was equivalent to making him second in command of the entire army. . . . I could not but feel that giving the command to him was equivalent to giving Washington to the rebels.[5]

Even Chase's account of his own expectation of disaster seems expressed moderately. In sharp contrast is Welles's description of the same incident:

Personal jealousies and professional rivalries, the bane and curse of armies, have entered deeply into ours.
    Stanton said in a suppressed voice, trembling with excitement, he was informed McClellan had been ordered to take command of the forces in Washington. General surprise was expressed. . . . Much was said. There was a more disturbed and desponding feeling than ever I witnessed in Council; the President was greatly distressed. . . .
    Chase earnestly and emphatically expressed his conviction that it would prove a national calamity.[6]

The whole first year of the diary is full of the same sort of material. Welles scoffed at the recurrent "rumors and speculations" about danger to Washington (1:139), and he was especially severe in criticizing those who put their own advantage ahead of that of the Union: "During the whole of this civil war, I have been beset and annoyed by interested patriots who had old steamers to sell which no one would buy" (1:496).
    Welles also (and often) complained about such selfish or egotistical behavior inside the Cabinet. For example, he complained about [Sec-

retary of State] Seward's "passion to be thought a master spirit in the Administration" (1:79), and in another entry he wrote that the "Rebel leaders understand Seward very well. He is fond of intrigue, of mystery, of sly, cunning management, and is easily led off on a wild chase by subtle fellows who can without difficulty excite his curiosity and flatter his vanity. Detectives, secret agents, fortune-tellers are his delight" (2:126). Similarly, he made fun of Secretary of War Stanton's desire to show his importance by being the first to leak news: "In these matters of announcing news he takes as deep an interest as in army movements which decide the welfare of the country" (1:365).

Welles was also critical of the failures of the Union Army: "Why cannot our army move as rapidly as the Rebels. The high water in the river has stopped them, yet our troops do not catch up. It has been the misfortune of our generals to linger, never to avail themselves of success" (1:367). But Welles was particularly sensitive to, and used his diary to complain about, the criticism he and his department received for failures by the Navy. In one incident Welles complained about the events that led to the escape of the Confederate ship *Tallahassee*. The blame, he insisted, belonged to one naval officer who had neglected Welles's orders to send a ship in pursuit, but also sent false information about the real situation, and to another who, encountering "wrecks and cargoes of the Confederate ship's victims," returned to port with the salvage instead of giving chase. "These fellows," Welles insisted, would "never wear an admiral's flag on the active list, or command a squadron in time of war" (2:110–15).

Welles also made sure to mention his own successes, vindicating decisions that had been criticized. In one entry he pointed to the correctness of his early support for the construction of ironclads: "The fight with the Merrimac made for them [the ironclads] rapid converts. When the first turret vessel, the Monitor, was building, many naval men and men in the shipping interests sneered at her as a humbug, and at me as no sailor or judge, until she vindicated her power and worth in that first remarkable conflict. Then I was abused by party men, because I hadn't made preparations for and built more" (1:495–96).

Welles was not universally critical of others. His view of Lincoln was relatively balanced. He described the president as "usually shrewd and sensible. . . . honest sincere, and confiding," and though he admitted that Lincoln had at times "mismanaged," Welles attributed these errors to the influence of some of Lincoln's advisors (2:130–31). Welles had a very high opinion of Admiral Farragut, a "real hero" who "sees to every movement, forms his line of battle with care and skill, puts himself at the head . . . if there is difficulty leads the way, regards no danger to himself, dashes by forts and overcomes obstructions." Welles was particularly impressed by the fact that, although a Virginian, Farragut left his "home and property . . . avowing openly and boldly, in the face and hearing of the Rebels by whom he was [then] surrounded, his determination to live and die owning allegiance to no flag but that of the Union under which he had served" (2:134).

Welles's diary includes few glimpses of his personal life and most of those, such as his reaction to his son's enlistment and departure for the army, are connected with the war:

To part with him has been painful to me beyond what I can describe. Were he older with more settled principles and habits, some of the anxieties which oppress me would be relieved. But he is a mere youth and has gone to the camp with boyish pride and enthusiasm and will be in danger of being misled when beyond a parent's control. He is just eighteen and goes alone on his mission. I have tried to dissuade him, but . . . when others were imperiling their lives and the lives of their children, how could I refrain and resist the earnest appeals of my son, whose heart was set on going. . . . I have attended closely to my duties, but I am sad and unfit for any labor. (2:82)

By the middle of 1864, long before the satisfactory conclusion of the war seemed assured, the federal government was already debating strategies for reconstruction, and this topic became one of the recurrent concerns in Welles's diary. He argued that punishing all Southerners would harm those who had never acted disloyally. Welles insisted that there should be "political equality" for all states; to do otherwise would be to "recognize the right and fact of secession" (2:84–85, 98–99).

Welles had predicted the conclusion of the war when he detected changes in the speeches by the "doves" (2:177). Finally, he recorded news of the evacuation of Petersburg, the capture of Richmond, and the surrender of Lee: "The tidings were spread over the country during the night and the country seems delirious with joy. Guns are firing, flags flying, men laughing, children cheering; all are jubilant. This surrender of the great Rebel captain and the most formidable and reliable army of the Secessionists virtually terminates the Rebellion" (2:272, 278).

Welles's joy was short-lived; he soon heard news of the assassination of Lincoln. Welles wrote a long two-day entry on the assassination, beginning with the first rumors in the night and continuing as he went with Stanton to the house across from Ford's Theater where Lincoln lay dying:

> We entered by ascending a flight of steps above the basement and passing through a long hall to the rear, where the President lay. . . . The giant sufferer lay extended diagonally across the bed, which was not long enough for him. He had been stripped of his clothes. His large arms which were occasionally exposed, were of a size which one would scarcely have expected from his spare appearance. His slow respiration lifted the [bed]clothes with each breath he took. His features were calm and striking. . . . About once an hour Mrs. Lincoln would repair to the bedside of her dying husband and with lamentation and tears remain till overcome by emotion. (2:283–88)

One of the most extensively treated subjects in the last years of the diary is the impeachment of President Johnson. Welles stressed principle over personality, and while his alliances with or opposition to certain individuals could be strongly personal, his defense of or attacks on personalities followed an assessment of their principles. His positive portrayal of Johnson and his negative treatment of Johnson's enemies, including Grant, grew as he came to see the president's political problems as the result of an attempt to uphold constitutional government.

As Welles became more concerned for the cause of President Johnson, he became more negative in his comments about General Grant, who he foresaw would "be the next President of the United States." Welles's initial concern was Grant's political inexperience. He did not believe that Grant would "disregard the Constitution," but that he had "no political principles, no intelligent idea of constitutional government" (3:15). Gradually, Welles started to question Grant's general competence, writing, "Whatever may be Grant's popularity growing out of military successes and services, I see no evidence of civil capacity, administrative ability, or general intelligence" (3:184). After Grant's nomination had made him an important opponent of the Johnson administration, Welles called Grant a man of "low instincts, a man of cunning . . . destitute of affection outside the family circle" (3:363).

Johnson narrowly escaped conviction, but Grant easily won the presidency, ending Welles's service as secretary of the Navy. His war was over, and his diary ended shortly after the change in administrations.

Chapter Four
War Diaries II—Civilian

Most of the best civilian diaries of the Civil War period were written by Southern women. One reason is that a large percentage of those men who had a strong interest in the war were engaged in military service. Another is that most of the war was fought in the South, and thus Southern civilians had more opportunity to observe it and more cause to fear its effects than did Northern ones.

But there are civilian diaries by Northerners that merit consideration. One of the best is that of Charlotte Forten, a young free black woman from Philadelphia who felt compelled to help her race by volunteering to teach newly freed slaves in the Sea Islands of South Carolina. Another notable civilian war diary is that of Adam Gurowski; however, as Gurowski was a recent immigrant, his diary can not really be classed as American.[1]

Five Southern women diarists stand out: Judith McGuire, Sarah Ida Fowler Morgan Dawson, Sarah Katherine Stone Holmes, Eliza Francis Andrews, and Mary Boykin Chesnut. Chesnut's diary has long been considered one of the greatest literary works to come out of the Civil War, as well as one of the greatest American diaries. However, the work that has received this praise, while written as if it were a true diary, is actually an extension and re-creation of Chesnut's real diary, much of which was destroyed during the war. Both versions will be considered in this chapter.

Judith W. McGuire (dates unknown)

Although Judith McGuire did not begin her habit of diary keeping because of the war, the portion that has been published under the title *Diary of a Southern Refugee* is very much a war diary. It does present some personal situations and sentiments not related to the war, but most of the entries are tied to it. One possible explanation for the limited focus of the diary may have resulted from the author's sense of privacy about her own life, a view supported by her assertion that the diary was not written for the public but for "a private record" kept "for members of the family who are too young to remember these days."[2] Indeed, the diary was first published anonymously. However, this factor seems not to have been as important as the overwhelming effect of the war, which drained much of the energy and interest she might have placed in personal concerns. In one entry McGuire expressed her conviction that the war had so affected Southern women that, although almost every one would "have her tale to tell" when the "cruel war" was over, few would be able to tell because life would have lost "its interest, its charm, even its hope" (219–20).

McGuire does provide enough information for the reader to assess her character. She was a reserved, religious, genteel, and "quiet elderly lady," not normally given to ostentatious behavior or emotional outbursts, and so her strong sentiments are often couched in language that seems formal and restrained. Yet her dedication to the Confederate cause and to her religious faith sometimes so overrode her reticence that she was moved to the other extreme, writing in a style that is excessively melodramatic. In one entry she wrote of the dead soldiers' spirits "wafted through clash and storm of battlefield to those peaceful joys" of heaven (43).

McGuire shows little inclination toward humor or self-criticism. For example, in one entry she describes the actions of the Reverend Dr. Pendleton, in whose character "the soldier and the chaplain are blended most harmoniously." In one battle the reverend commanded an artillery piece covering the retreat of some Confederate troops, and "whenever he ordered its discharge he was heard to say, reverently, 'The Lord have mercy on their souls—fire!'" McGuire wrote that she was not fully "reconciled to the clergy going upon the field as soldiers," but she seems to have been unaware that there might be something ironic in his blessing or in her own declaration that "the result was almost miraculous" (34).

For McGuire, religion and patriotism were inseparable, and she saw the Confederate army as defending "The Southern Church" from "the hosts who are now desecrating her hallowed precincts" (179–80). She believed that God was on the side of the South and was pleased that many of the Southern leaders were "God fearing men" and "professing Christians" (261). When a wounded soldier expressed his concern that God might not favor their side because many Yankees "are Christians and pray as hard as we do," she answered him, "God will hear us for the justice of our cause" (98).

From the first, she believed that justice would insure victory and that the South should maintain an optimistic position in the face of what appeared to be overwhelming odds. She attacked the "croakers," pessimists who would "roll their gloomy eyes" and cast doubt on the wisdom of the war and its conduct (112):

Some of our old men are a little nervous, look doubtful and talk of the impotency of the South. Oh I feel utter scorn for such remarks. We must not admit weakness. Our soldiers do not think of weakness; they know our hearts are strong, and their hands well skilled in the use of the rifle. . . . Their hearts feel strong when they think of the justice of their cause. In that is *our* hope. (13)

Even after major defeats at Vicksburg and Gettysburg, she looked toward each encounter with a hope born of her conviction that "the God of battles is with us" (259).

McGuire could even find hope in a series of Southern losses which, she declared, might "make chicken hearted men and women despondent, but to the true and brave it gives a fresh stimulus for exertion." In one entry she wrote about meeting "two young Kentuckians" who, coming to enlist in the Confederate army, had become convinced by the people they saw "lounging about the Exchange" that Virginia was "ready to give up" (108). McGuire reacted forcefully to counter that impression:

All the blood in my system boiled in an instant. "Where, sir," said I, "have you seen Virginians ready to give up their cause? . . . do you suppose that Virginians worthy of the name are now seen lounging about the Exchange? There you see the idlers and shirkers of the whole Southern army. No true man under forty-five is to be found there. Virginia, sir is in the camp. Go there and find the true men of the South. . . . There you will find the chivalry of the South; and if Virginia does not receive you with the shout of enthusiasm which you anticipated, it is because the fire burns steadily and deeply. The surface blaze has long ago passed away." (108–9)

Such rhetoric is typical of McGuire, and her record shows that she was not alone in her patriotism.

McGuire's record of battle itself is limited because so much of what she recorded was secondhand information. She did see some skirmishing and was present at the fall of Richmond, but she witnessed few battles. Early in the diary she waited for corroboration before recording events because, she claimed, she "didn't want to record any thing which . . . [she] didn't *know* to be true." However, she soon gave over a major portion of her account to whispered rumors and newspaper reports (46). For example, in one entry she wrote, "General Lee was heard to say to General Jackson, 'The fighting is desperate; can our men stand it?' Jackson replied, 'General, I know our boys—they will never give back'" (125). The language used here seems more the stuff of legend than of history.

Fortunately, McGuire was close to many of the events of the war, and she was associated with a number of figures in or connected to the army or government (for example, she reported having breakfast with Robert E. Lee) and gained a good deal of her information about the war from them. Her home in Arlington was just across from Washington and was, therefore, a target for occupation by Union forces. She described her emotions in leaving: "As I looked at the Capitol in the distance I could scarcely believe my senses. That Capitol of which I had always been so proud! Can it be possible that it is no longer *our* Capitol? And are our countrymen under its eaves making mighty preparation to drain our hearts' blood? . . . Why can not we part in peace?" (10–11). The McGuires were unwilling to leave their home, but a threat to arrest all Secessionists finally forced them to become "refugees," a label that, in her hope to return, Mrs. McGuire was reluctant to accept.

McGuire does a good job of describing the plight of her fellow refugees. Housing was only one of their many problems. Some Southern families welcomed the refugees, "Pallets [were] spread on the floor; every sofa and couch *sheeted* for visitors of whom they never heard before," but lodgings were a constant problem (173). The McGuires were repeatedly forced to accept inadequate accommodations, such as kitchenless apartments and damp basement rooms, and even when appropriate lodgings were available, they were often too expensive.

Yet, as McGuire's diary shows the reader, the refugees were not the only Southern civilians to suffer from the war. She records the burning of homes and the mistreatment of civilians so that her "children's children may know what we suffer during this unnatural war" (297). Early in the war the hardship suffered by the Southern women was minimal. They had to forgo desserts and wine, to extend their coffee with grain, and to give up the "handsome bonnets, wrappings and silk dressings . . . [that] once they considered absolutely necessary to their wardrobes" (81–82). McGuire showed that "the Southern women were as ingenious as the men were brave" (185–86); they made boots from sail canvas and ink from elderberries (251–52). Southern women sacrificed more than the loss of fashion. McGuire's diary shows such a willingness to sacrifice in her record of a conversation with a "heroine in homespun," a woman who had already sent three sons into the army and was now preparing for the departure of her husband:

"Well, he's fifty-four years old, but he's well and hearty like, and ought to do something for his country. So he says to me, says he, 'The country wants men; I wonder if I could stand marching; I've a great mind to try.' Says I, 'Old man, I don't think you could, you would break down; but I tell you what you can do—you can drive a wagon in the place of a young man that's driving, and the young man can fight.' Says he, 'So I will' . . . I shall miss him mightily; but I aint never cried about it." (99)

Such anecdotes capturing both the language and the feeling of the time are among the best parts of McGuire's work.

McGuire kept up her patriotic enthusiasm through loss after loss. Even after Richmond fell and Lee surrendered she could not bring herself to admit defeat: "Not yet—I cannot feel that all is over yet." Only with the surrender of the last major Confederate army could she close her diary with the line "My native land, good-night!" (360).

Sarah Ida Fowler Morgan Dawson (1842–1909)

Several of the best Southern women diarists aspired to become professional writers. Dawson worked as a journalist and translator; Andrews and Chesnut wrote novels. Yet, despite her literary interests, Mrs. Dawson had never intended to have her diary made public and had even prepared instructions to have it burned after her death. However, her son, who was to become its first editor, finally persuaded her to preserve it.[3] The versions finally published, while incomplete, are without corrupting alterations.

She began her diary on March 9, 1862, in a way that suggests she had begun writing as a means of alleviating boredom: "Here I am at your service, Madame Idleness, waiting for any suggestion it may please you to put in my weary brain as a means to pass this dull cloudy Sunday afternoon" (1). Despite this claim, there is evidence that her diary, like so many others, sprang from tension rather than relaxation.

In the second entry she admits that she had been going through a particularly distressing period. She claims that until the previous year she had been "a happy, careless child who danced through life, loving God's whole world" with "no idea of sorrow or grief" (4). Then suddenly her brother was killed in a duel, her father died, and, as the diary began, the Northern army was approaching her home.[4] These three "tragedies" have to be considered together in assessing her record. While much of the subject matter and the period covered by the diary seem dictated by the Civil War, the focus and controlling force of the diary is the author's sense of family.

On February 5, 1864, Miss Morgan received the news that one of her brothers had died; then six days later she learned that a second had died: "Dead! Dead! Both dead! O my brothers! What have we lived for except you? We, who would so gladly have laid down our lives for yours, are left desolate to mourn over all we loved and hoped for, weak and helpless; while you, so strong, noble, and brave, have gone before us without a murmur" (426). The family found these deaths especially painful because they came without warning. The Morgans had counted on divine protection and suddenly found their "faith" was only "presumption" (427). As the letters came announcing death after death, her sister Miriam fell "raving on the ground," wildly shrieking, while her mother lay so insensible that "only fearful moans showed she was alive" (430–31). Sarah was denied the full expression of her own grief as she had to care for her family; she even had to keep from the others the special sadness that would come from learning that the death of one of her brothers had, in part, resulted from a misdiagnosis by his physicians (432).

Miss Morgan survived this ordeal, but her diary did not. It seems to end with comments on the fall of the Confederacy and the assassination of Lincoln, but they only tie up one part of the diary's story. We also learn of her brother's engagement, her sister's departure, and her own entry into a new career as a teacher. This concluding section also presents the last in a long series of contrasts between innocent hope and the reality born of harsh experience. She writes of thinking back to a ball that she had attended the year before and recalling that "all of those dancing there that night have undergone trial and affliction since" (7). At the end, she contrasts the few troops who were returning to the regiments that had left years before. In one telling entry she writes of an unexpected encounter on a train with Mr. Todd, a childhood friend who had become a Union soldier: "The Mr. Todd who was my 'sweetheart' when I was twelve and he twenty-four, who was my brother's friend, and daily at our home, was put away from our acquaintance at the beginning of the war. This one, I should not know. Cords of candy and mountains of bouquets bestowed in childish days will not make my country's enemy my friend now that I am a woman" (439).

Sarah Katherine Stone Holmes (1841–1907)

One of the most common motives for keeping a diary is the hope that it will allow the diarist to relive the past. In a preface written in 1900 Mrs. Holmes (then Miss Stone) described the partial fulfillment of that motive: "In looking over the yellowing pages and the fading writing of my old diary . . . how the old life comes back, the gay busy life of the Plantation at Brokenburn with Mamma, a beautiful, brilliant woman of thirty-seven at the head . . . [and me at nineteen] the much indulged young lady of the house."[5] It is fitting that the editor of Holmes's diary titled it *Brokenburn,* after the Stones' Louisiana plantation. Even though much of the diary was written during a long exile in Texas and its existence seems to have been determined by the war, it is really the record of the end of a way of life, symbolized by that plantation.[6]

The diary began as Holmes's brother rushed to enlist fearing "that the fighting will be over before he can get there" (13). The diarist's own exuberance is reflected in her language "Throughout the length and breadth of the land the trumpet of war is sounding, and from every hamlet and village, from city and country, men are hurrying by thousands, eager to be led to battle against Lincoln's hordes" (14). But less than nine months later she was writing, "The manner in which the North is moving her forces, now that she thinks us surrounded and can give us the annihilating blow, reminds me of a party of hunters crouched around the covert of the deer, and when the lines are drawn and there is no escape, they close in and kill" (85).

Holmes, like so many civilians in the early stages of a war, expressed a dissatisfaction at her own "inactive" life when there was such stir and excitement in the busy world outside. Her wish was "to be in the heat and turmoil of it all, to live, to live, not stagnate here" (87). Unfortunately, Holmes had her wish granted, but not as she wished. The war first came to Brokenburn in an order by the Confederate army to burn the cotton on the plantation to keep it out of the hands of the

Union forces that had taken New Orleans and were threatening to control the whole Mississippi River: "As far as we can see are the ascending wreaths of smoke. . . . Though agreeing on the necessity of destroying the cotton, all regret it. And it has thrown a gloom over the country that nothing but a great victory could lighten" (100–1).

Soon the area surrounding Brokenburn was in Union hands. "Living in constant dread of great danger, not knowing what form it . . . [might] take, and [feeling] utterly helpless," Holmes's family left their plantation on March 25, 1863 (185–86). Most of the balance of the diary was written during their "exile" in Texas. Holmes's descriptive skill is evident in passages such as the following, showing the trials of the numerous refugees:

The scene beggars description: such crowds of Negroes of all ages and sizes, wagons, mules, horses, dogs, baggage, and furniture of every description, very little of it packed. It was just thrown in promiscuous heaps—pianos, tables, chairs . . . with soldiers, drunk and sober, combing over it all, shouting and laughing. While thronging everywhere were refugees—men women and children—everybody and everything trying to get on the cars, all fleeing from the Yankees or worse still, the Negroes. (191)

While refugees, Holmes and her family were robbed by black Union soldiers, one of whom threatened the diarist with a pistol, and "fleeced" by local Southerners, who charged them $3000 to rent a wagon to go four miles (94–96). However, for Holmes the worst suffering came when she learned of the death of two of her brothers.

Even after Lee's defeat, Holmes tried to counter those who argued for surrender, writing, "I say, 'Never, never, though we perish in the track of their endeavor!'" But such protests, she admitted, were "words, idle words. What can poor weak women do?" (333–34). Her reason for this stubborn refusal to admit the fall of the Confederacy was not only patriotism, but also her attempt to deny that the sacrifices of her brothers had been wasted:

The best and bravest of the South sacrificed—and for nothing. Yes, worse than nothing. Only to rivet more firmly the chains that bind us. The bitterness of death is in the thought. We could bear the loss of my brave little brothers when we thought that they had fallen at the post of duty defending their Country, but now to know that those glad, bright spirits suffered and toiled in vain, that the end is overwhelming defeat, the thought is unendurable. (340)

In November, 1865, Mrs. Holmes returned to Brokenburn, and her diary shows that life was already starting to return to the plantation. But she wrote only two entries that month (one includes an amusing comment on the man who would become her future husband), another almost two years later (after an incident in which one of her brothers shot a field hand), and two more in 1868. The diary did not really survive the return to Brokenburn with its reminders of what had been. As Mrs. Holmes explained, much had changed and the plantation did not "seem the same place" (364).

Eliza Frances Andrews (1840–1931)

After the period covered by her diary, Fanny Andrews began to write professionally, publishing several novels under the pen name Elzey Hay (*Prince Hal or The Romance of a Rich Young Man, A Family Secret, A Mere Adventurer*) in addition to a number of stories, essays, and poems.[7] Even in the diary, she looks at her world with a novelist's eye, searching her experiences for material that might be shaped into a novel. Andrews's writing experience led her to edit her diary for publication, and, by her own admission, in the process she eliminated some material, including "tiresome reflections and silly flirtations" (viii). As a result the surviving work is less complete than a serious diary reader might wish.

The Andrews family was "divided in politics." Like Mrs. Morgan's father, Andrews's father was a firm Unionist, "almost the only man in Georgia who stood out openly for the Union" (172, 220). However, his sentiments did not prevent his children from supporting and fighting on the side of the Confederacy. Indeed, to some extent the diary is a tale of two struggles, one a war within a nation, the other a struggle within a family.

Andrews's rebellion from and only partial reconciliation with her father's position paralleled those of the South and the North. Late in the diary she claimed that she had not always been a "red-hot secessionist" but, like her father, she had hoped that war might be prevented. However, elsewhere in the diary she recounts how in secret rebellion she had helped to sew "the first rebel flag" in their city. The diary seems to have emerged from that period in which the destruction wrought by Sherman's march allowed her to abandon any pretense to "see a certain tragic grandeur in the spectacle of the Great Republic struggling desperately for its existence" (214, 313–14). Andrews did not glorify war and tried to show "what a horrible thing war is when stripped of all its 'pomp and circumstance!'" Nevertheless, her diary leaves little doubt about where her loyalty lay (79).

The surviving portion of Andrews's diary was begun in December, 1864, and lasted only nine months; however, it is still substantial, consisting of full and regular entries. In the first of these she describes her trip across the "burnt country" with its "Sherman's sentinels," the charred chimneys of the buildings destroyed during the passage of the Union Army. She writes that there was no food there except for some grain that the Union soldiers dropped in feeding their horses and even that was being picked over by Confederate troops in the area who had been reduced to eating "raw turnips, meat skins and parched corn" (32–33). Even the railroad had been wrecked, its track "torn up and the iron twisted into every conceivable shape. Some of it was wrapped round the trunks of trees as if the cruel invaders, not satisfied with doing all the injury they could to their fellowmen, must spend their malice on the innocent trees of the forest, whose only fault was that they grew on Southern soil" (47). So great was the devastation that Andrews was willing to excuse those Southerners who admitted to "losing" (a euphemism for executing) Union prisoners (30–33).

Parallel to the depredations of the invading Yankees were "the horrors of the stockade" at Andersonville. Andrews tells of shuddering as she passed its gate and saw "the seething mass of humanity inside, like a swarm of blue flies crawling over a grave." Though she declared the prison "a blot on the fair name of the Confederacy," she blamed it on the "cruel monsters" of the North who had "brought it all on themselves . . . by refusing to exchange prisoners" (64–65). Hearing descriptions of prisoners living in "underground huts . . . alive with vermin," lying "on the ground in their own excrements," Dying "at the rate of 150 a day" many "without a rag to lie on or a garment to cover them," Andrews wrote that her heart ached "for the poor wretches," and expressed her fear that God would "suffer some terrible retribution to fall upon us for letting such things happen." Nevertheless, she still maintained that the Confederacy, its own soldiers "starving in the field," could provide nothing more and, therefore, continued to assert, "the Yankees themselves are really more to blame than we" (78–79).

When she could, Andrews tried to turn away from such depressing subjects and to write about parties and romance or to make practical jokes about invading enemies.[8] But, as the fighting drew closer, she saw signs of panic: soldiers blundering "in the dark fighting pretty much at random" and the widespread acceptance of "rumors of Lee's surrender." "The common cry" had become: "'It is useless to struggle longer' . . . the poor wounded men go hobbling about the streets with despair on their faces. There is a new pathos in a crutch or an empty sleeve, now, that we know it was all for nothing" (146, 154–55).

When news of the surrender finally came, Andrews was resigned but unchanged in her patriotism: "I am crushed and bowed down to the earth, in sorrow, but not in shame. No! I am more of a rebel today than ever I was when things looked brightest for the Confederacy." Indeed, her anger seems almost as strongly against hypocritical Southerners as it is against the Yankees: "It makes me furious to see how many Union men are cropping up everywhere, and how few there are, to hear them talk now, who really approved of secession" (172).

Over half the diary was written after the fall of the Confederacy, as the "shattered remains of Lee's army" began to return (181). Andrews wrote that "nobody seems to care about anything anymore." The "chaos and demoralization" of the South had become so widespread that when "a Texas regiment" began rioting over rations, it was soon "joined by all the disorderly elements" in plundering the quartermaster's stores (193–94). For Andrews these disturbances were not as troublesome as the actions of Union soldiers, such as one troop of cavalry she saw ride by with "bags of plunder tied to their saddlebags." Still more threatening seemed the behavior of the freed slaves, especially those who had joined the Union army: "Think of it! Bringing armed negroes here to threaten and insult us."[9] More than any other action by the blacks, it was what she considered their "insolence" that Andrews most frequently found objectionable. She upbraided those blacks who "deserted" their former masters, but was not at ease even with those who remained loyal, worrying that "every black man" might be "a possible spy" (343).

Andrews documented the way that the fear and anger of the Southern whites began to prompt atrocities. In one incident two white men were "accused of murdering an old negro woman because she left her master's plantation to go off and try the blessings of freedom. . . . One of the men is said to have shot her, while the other broke her ribs and beat her on the head with a stone till she died" (341). Andrews wrote about another killing involving "a party of young men" who, hearing that some blacks were planning "a secret meeting which was suspected of boding no good to the whites . . . went out to break it up." Andrews's prejudice is apparent in her unquestioning acceptance of the excuse that the killing was unintentional: "One of the boys, to frighten them [the blacks], shot off his gun and accidentally killed a woman. He didn't mean to hurt anybody, but the Yankees vow they will hang the whole batch" (343). The diary ended before the period that Andrews later called "the still blacker darkness of reconstruction"; but it already contained elements that would trouble the South long into the future (385).

Mary Boykin Chesnut (1823–1886)

Ever since 1905, when an excerpted version of Mary Boykin Chesnut's account of the Civil War was published posthumously under the title *Diary from Dixie,* the work has been hailed as one of the finest records of the war, a source of important information about the war as experienced by Southern civilians and a work of high literary merit. However, while based on the private diary she had kept during the war, the bulk of *Diary from Dixie* was actually written twenty years later, between 1881 and her death in 1884. The only portions of the wartime diary that survived cover February 18–December 8, 1861, January or early February–February 23, and early May–June 26, 1865.

In 1875 Chesnut, who had already been trying to write a number of novels, attempted to revise her wartime "journal"; however, she abandoned that project the following year. Five years later she again attempted to work with the journal materials, but this time she took far more license in both style and content. She not only developed entries of the original diary, but also included a considerable amount of new material. At the time of her death she had not yet brought the work to the stage she would have considered appropriate for publication, but she had produced a unique and important document. Thanks to the fine scholarship of C. Vann Woodward and Elisabeth Muhlenfeld we now have not only a complete version of this work and an excellent edition of the surviving portions of the original diary, but also an understanding of their true natures, relationship, and development.[10]

Woodward's edition of *Diary from Dixie,* entitled *Mary Chesnut's Civil War,* integrates some material from the original and the re-created diaries. The contrast is often revealing. In one entry in the re-created diary Chesnut talks of an enthusiastic speech by the Confederate president, declaring, "He is an old war horse—and scents the battlefield from afar" (*M,* 109). However, in the contemporaneous diary she also noted, "The President took all the credit to himself for the victory.

Said the wounded roused & shouted for Jeff Davis—& the men rallied at the sight of him & rushed on & routed the enemy. The truth is, Jeff Davis was not two miles from the battlefield—but he is greedy for military fame" (P, 103).

Despite the fact that Chesnut revised for publication, even in that revised version she was true to the diary form in more than appearance. She preserved the immediate perspective of the diary even when she could have made her evidence more accurate by altering it. For example, she created a conversation in which she is asked, "Why do you write in your diary at all, if, as you say, you have to contradict everyday what you wrote yesterday?" Chesnut's answer is, "Because I tell the tale as it is told to me. I write current rumor. I do not vouch for anything" (M, 163). In preserving this sense of rumor Chesnut was able to give a better picture of the situation of civilians, who were affected by false rumors as surely as the soldiers in the field were affected by bullets.

Chesnut began her diary with an attempt to quell her concerns about the coming conflict and her sense that, while she would "always regret that [she] . . . had not kept a journal during the two past delightful and eventful years," the coming period would prove still more worthy of record: "I do not allow myself vain regrets or sad foreboding. This southern Confederacy must be supported now by calm determination—& cool brains. We have risked all, and we must play our best for the stake is life or death." In this spirit Chesnut prepared to record "with some distinctness the daily shocks" (P, 3). She may also have considered the diary an aid to memory. Chesnut took opiates for headaches and other problems, and one side-effect was a weakening of memory. Resuming her diary in 1865 after a lapse, she wrote "I must regain the habit of regular writing in my journal. Will be worthless—for I forget everything if I neglect it a day" (P, 221).

Chesnut viewed political and social issues as a part of those experiences that belonged in a personal diary, and she was particularly well placed and well prepared to begin such a record. Her father had been "a South Carolina Nullifier—Governor of the state at the time of the N[ullification] row" (P, 4), and both he and her husband had served as United States senators.[11] However, while the diarist claimed that she "was of necessity a rebel born" and from a state "so rampant" that no one could live there "unless he was a fire eater," Chesnut approached the conflict with some ambivalence. On the one hand, she wanted the South "to fight & stop talking," on the other she had misgivings about the outcome, "feeling a nervous dread & horror of this break with so great a power as U.S.A." (*P,* 4).

Chesnut's picture of the war as experienced by Southern women is tragic; death constantly intrudes. In one entry she writes of having had "a merry time" with "so many witty sayings said" at dinner at the home of the president of the Confederacy, and then moves immediately to the suffering of a woman who had lost her husband in the war: "His wife lies quiet. To day as a solemn touching military funeral went by, the first sound she heard of the dead march, she fainted!" (*P,* 101).

Since most of the Southern defeats came in the period not covered in the extant original diary, that work has comparatively few entries about death and suffering; but the dead haunt the re-created diary. Writing of a period in which she spent her mornings working with the wounded in the hospital, Chesnut tells how she would be troubled for the rest of the day and night with memories of "loathsome wounds, distortion, stumps of limbs exhibited to all and not half cured" (*M,* 641). Even when writing of an hour of leisure spent sitting with her husband in the sunshine, she recalls the funeral of one of Jefferson Davis's children, an experience that so disturbed her that she seemed to see the "dark sorrow stricken figures" rise before her like ghosts (*M,* 608–9). There are many such contrasts between rejoicing and mourning. As one of her acquaintances remarked, even those women who had not lost a husband or lover in the war may have been doomed to spinsterhood, their "possible husbands and lovers killed before . . . [they] even so much as knew them" (*M,* 523). Each romantic or humorous anecdote about a courtship, and there are many in the diary, is set against a background of past tragedy, present suffering, or future danger.

Chesnut showed her awareness that suffering was not restricted to Southern women. Looking through a "portfolio from the field of battle—filled with letters from *hard* Yankee women," including "one from a man to his sweetheart 'thrilling with her last embrace,'" Chesnut expressed her realization that these hated Yankees were still "*women,* wives and mothers" (*P,* 103). In the revised diary she added: "Women are the same everywhere" (*M,* 108).

The war is the most frequent and important topic of the diaries, but others such as slavery are prominent. Though slavery was crucial to the conflict between North and South, Chesnut's diary argues that it was not the only issue leading to the war. The re-created diary refers to Southerners, even those highly placed in the Confederate government, who were against the continuation of slavery but fought for "Southern rights" for protection from domination by "those nasty Yankees" (M, 344). Chesnut cites the example of one minister who thanked God from the pulpit that "Slavery is doomed the world over," but who still supported the Confederacy to preserve "the freedom to govern our own country as we see fit" (M, 644). She also tried to bolster her position by asserting that slavery was not financially viable (M, 803). However, such material, written after the war, might be dismissed as an attempt to defend the South's claim to higher motives for its rebellion. Chesnut insisted that both she and her husband hated slavery and believed it a morally indefensible, outdated institution. She pronounced one letter she had written in 1842 "the most fervid abolition document I have ever read" (M, 246), and made a point of insisting that the only slave she and her husband ever bought was the husband of her maid and that that purchase had only been made to prevent him from being sold out of the region.

Chesnut did not deny that some mistreatment of slaves occurred, but she claimed that such mistreatment was the exception. One extreme case she cited in the re-created diary was that of Adam McWillie, "a savage," long dead who was said to have "put negroes in hogsheads with nails driven in all around it and rolled the poor things downhill." Chesnut recorded the belief by the negroes that "the devil would not have him in hell, he was too bad. So his spirit is roaming about where he made a little hell of his own while he was alive." While indicting "old Adam," Chesnut seems to have felt compelled to suggest that he was an exception by concluding this passage with the statement that his son "was an amiable person" (M, 776).

For Chesnut, the mistreatment of slaves was just one of the injustices that those in power inflict upon those they control. Though the writings of other diarists covered in this volume argue to the contrary, Chesnut claimed that Southern women generally opposed slavery, and that the institution survived through the baser impulse of Southern men. Woodward makes an effective argument that Chesnut's antislavery was jut part of a general feminist indictment of a masculine tyranny that kept women, "like the slaves . . . subject to the absolute authority of the patriarchal system" by citing her statement that "all married women, all children and girls who live in their fathers' houses are slaves" (M, li).

In two successive sentences in the re-created diary, Chesnut yoked slavery with the harsh treatment of children: "I hate slavery. I even hate the harsh authority I see parents think it their duty to exercise *toward their children*" (*P*, 246). In another entry she compared the beating of a slave in *Uncle Tom's Cabin* to the beating of a deformed child in Dickens's *Nicholas Nickleby* (*P*, 381). Her belief in the slave owners' paternalism can be seen in her claim that Southern slave owners did not gain from their slaves but really served them: "All that had been gained by it [slavery] goes to the North and the negroes." Most Southern slave owners, she maintained, were good; indeed, they were "martyrs" who sacrificed their wealth to "support a horde of idle, dirty Africans" (*P*, 246–47).

Such language is just one indication that Chesnut's opposition to slavery did not mean that she was free of racial prejudice. She might question the right of whites to own blacks, but never the white man's superiority. She denied the existence of characters like Harriet Beecher Stowe's Eva, the saintly white child in *Uncle Tom's Cabin* who tried to aid mistreated blacks, not only because Chesnut thought such mistreatment was rare, but also because she didn't believe that "people can love things ugly and repulsive simply because they ought to do so" (*P*, 308). Similarly she denied the possibility of "an interesting book with a negro heroine down here" insisting that Southerners know that "Those beastly negress beauties [are] animals" (*M*, 243). As an example of this "beastliness" Chesnut tells an anecdote about Martha Adamson, "a beautiful mulatress" who "to the amazement of everybody, married a coal black negro." When the woman was asked how being "so nearly white . . . could she marry that horrid negro?" her answer was that she inherited "the taste of her white father" for her black mother. Chesnut's response that the answer showed the woman's coarseness, reveals her own inability to see the impropriety of the question that the woman was made to answer. Chesnut took her own assumption of the superiority of white beauty for granted, going so far as to qualify her own statement about the woman's beauty by adding that, while she was "as good looking as ever they [mulattos] are to me, I have never seen a mule as handsome as a horse" (*P*, 243).

Martha Adamson's response is especially important because it points to the miscegenation that undercut the slaveholders' pretensions to morality in enslaving blacks. In one of the earliest entries in the diary Chesnut wrote of a black woman on the auction block:

I saw today a sale of Negroes—Mulatto women in *silk dresses*—one girl was on the stand. Nice looking . . . She looked as coy & pleased at the bidder.

South Carolina slave holder as I am my very soul sickened—it is too dreadful. I tried to reason—this is not worse than the willing sale most women make of themselves in marriage—nor can the consequences be worse. The Bible authorizes marriage and slavery—poor women! poor slaves! (*P*, 21)

Chesnut's sickness is more the result of her perception of the sexual use the sale implied than her objection to selling a human being. In the revised version she added that "women sell themselves and are sold in marriage, from queens downward," but this assertion seems not to have been fully comforting (*M*, 15). Indeed, in an entry in the original diary written only two weeks after that above Chesnut wrote:

I wonder if it be a sin to think slavery a curse to any land. Sumner said not one word of this hated institution which is not true.[12] Men & women are punished when their masters and mistresses are brutes & not when they do wrong—& then we live surrounded by prostitutes. An abandoned woman is sent out of any decent house elsewhere. Who thinks any worse of a Negro or Mulatto woman for being a thing we can't name? God forgive *us*, but ours is a *monstrous* system. . . . Good women we have, *but* they talk of all *nastiness*—tho they never do wrong. (*P*, 42)

Slavery had affected not only such female slaves, but also the white slave owners who used them. Expanding on this concern in the revised diary, Chesnut argued that these slave owners were *debased* not only by their sexual misconduct, but also because of the hypocrisy that they maintained. The slave owner who ran "a hideous black harem" in his own home would still pretend to be "the best husband, father and member of the church in the world," while his wife and daughters would pretend that they do not even "dream what is as plain before their eyes as the sunlight . . . [and] play their parts of unsuspecting angels to the letter" (*M*, 168–69).

Despite a prejudice against blacks, Chesnut gave numerous examples of black slaves displaying a high degree of virtue. They were brave, loving, loyal, and honorable. At Bull Run a slave "rushed in the midst of the fight" to bring food to his "*tired* & hungry Massa" (*P*, 112). Such examples support her position that the behavior of the blacks was not just prompted by the fear of retribution. In her *Private Diary* she wrote of a former slave who, "living very comfortably" after the fall of the Confederacy, called on his former master "to offer his assistance & protection" (*P*, 239). She claimed that although the freed blacks showed a "natural and exultant joy at being free," there was "not a single case of a negro who betrayed his master" (*M*, 801, 803).

Though she repeatedly insisted that having lived so long and so closely with blacks, she and other white Southerners had a special ability to understand them, Chesnut searched for, but was unable to fathom, the blacks' motives. Even in the hindsight of the revised diary she inserted a passage in which she first wrote that she could not understand why the slaves did not seize the opportunity to flee to freedom in the North and later, when a black who had been well treated did try to escape, she claimed not to be able to understand why he did so.

Chesnut did have a sense of the motives of the white Southerners and their fierce patriotism, and despite her opposition to slavery and her early fears about the war she was loyal to the South. She repeatedly contrasted the attitudes of many of her friends who were eager for the war with her own sense of its potential costs. She seemed to sense that the eradication of slavery would have far less effect on the way of life she and her friends enjoyed than the war would.

There is a subtle but significant difference between Chesnut's two diary accounts of her reaction to the start of the war. In the revised diary she stressed her fears about the conflict that she was sure would come. She wrote of watching her friends enjoying all the world had to offer: beautiful and charming company, "English grouse . . . venison from the west, salmon from the lakes," and called their gaiety, "as madly jolly as the sailors who break into the strong room when the ship is going down" (*M*, 39–40). In the original diary Chesnut herself was one of those having "the merriest time," unable to "imagine *war* began today" (*P*, 58).

Chesnut's original diary of 1861 ends without any great fear for the rebellion, but the doubts expressed early in the re-created diary grow until, only a year into the war, most signs of the early exuberance have passed, and Chesnut can write of "battle after battle, disaster after disaster. Every morning's paper enough to kill a well woman [or] age a strong and hearty one" (*P*, 327). Under the date April 27, 1862, just after the fall of New Orleans, Chesnut wrote that she believed that the Confederacy was "lost," "gone," and "done to death by the politicians" who cared more about squabbling over "precedence" than for their country (*P*, 330).

Such internal struggles form a major theme in the re-created diary, but are not at all clear in the original. Chesnut tried to blame this internal bickering and search for personal advancement for the failure of the Confederacy, and suggested that, unlike the calculating Yankees, too many Southerners assumed that theirs would be a "rosewater revolution," like those in romantic novels, and so were unprepared for the "hideous agony" of the real war (*M*, 339). She suggested that too many Southerners doubted that the Yankees had the "courage" and "willingness to fight," preferring to believe that when the practical Yankees saw they couldn't make the war pay, they would "let it alone." And she argued that too few realized or were willing to accept the proposition that, though the Southerners might "do all that can be done by pluck and muscle, endurance, and dogged courage—dash and red-hot patriotism," the war would be a long fight against great odds with no certain success at the end of it (*M*, 83–87).

By the middle of 1864 the prospect of a Northern victory had become increasingly evident. The entries of this section of the re-created diary are filled with talk of dead soldiers and broken spirits. Chesnut claimed that her concerns led at least one friend to whom she showed her diary to call her a "Cassandra"—after the Trojan prophetess of disaster who, despite the accuracy of her predictions, could not get her countrymen to believe her (*M*, 674–76).

The final section of the original diary covers the end of the Confederacy and the attempt of those around Chesnut to assign blame for their defeat and deal with the victorious Yankees. She wrote:

> There is one universal hue & cry. This one caused our failure—the other one— here—there—everywhere. I say every man who failed to do his utter most aided—every man who could & did not fight caused it. I do not see that any did their duty but the dead heroes—the wounded & maimed—& those sturdy souls who first went into it—& were found at their post under arms when the *generals* gave them up to the Yankees. (*P*, 247)

While Chesnut herself had long predicted disaster, she continued to ◄ insist that even with its tragic end the rebellion was preferable to peaceful submission to the North. Numerous fiction writers as well as several historians have romanticized the Civil War, emphasizing its symbolic and epic qualities. Chesnut cherished this vision of the war both in the re-created *Diary from Dixie* and in the *Private Diary*, which reflected her contemporaneous attitude.

Charlotte L. Forten (1838–1914)

Charlotte Forten was a black woman, and the racial issues so important to the Civil War formed an important part of her life and diary.

As the editor of the *Journal* notes in his introduction, "no other influence was so strong in shaping Charlotte Forten's thoughts."[13] Yet the
first section comprising almost half of the extant diary began in 1854
when she was a sixteen-year-old schoolgirl in Salem, Massachusetts,
and the motives she announced in commencing the diary were, like
those of most diarists, unrelated to race: "A wish to record the passing
events of my life, which even if quite unimportant to others, naturally
possess great interest to myself," a practice that she hoped would offer
"a pleasant and profitable employment" as well as "pleasure in later
years" (42).

Forten's record includes the expression of religious feelings and concerns about personal inadequacy typical of spiritual journals:

I have been thinking lately very much about death—that strange mysterious
awful reality. . . . Oh! I long to be good to be able to meet death calmly and
fearlessly, strong in faith and holiness. But this can only be through the One
who died for us, through the pure and perfect love of Him, who was all
holiness and love. But how can I be worthy of His love while I still cherish
this feeling toward my enemies, this unforgiving spirit? (57)

Other entries are typical of those in romance and courtship diaries: "I
am *lonely* tonight. I long for one earnest sympathizing soul to be in
close communion with my own. I long for the pressure of a loving
hand in mine, the touch of loving lips upon my aching brow. I long
to lay my weary head upon an earnest heart, which beats for me,—to
which I am dearer than all the world beside" (124). Forten possessed
an active and capable mind, and her diary offers an interesting portrait
of social, cultural, and educational activities.

Such entries might have filled her diary had Forten been white; however, though Forten did not plan to deal with racial problems, she
could not exclude race from her diary any more than she could exclude
it from her life. She dreamt of escape; a picture of a church in England
made her long to go there, not just to see it, but also because it seemed
so distant from America, "my native land where I am hated and op-
pressed because God has given me a *dark skin*" (54). The diary seems
formed by the tension between two modes of existence: the life she
wanted and was suited to by virtue of her abilities and the life she lived
because of prejudice.

This tension is apparent by the second entry. She explains that,
while she had not intended to make an entry that evening, she has
"just heard of something which is worth recording;—something which

must ever rouse in the mind of every true friend of liberty and humanity, feelings of the deepest indignation and sorrow. Another fugitive from bondage has been arrested . . . [and denied] the freedom which he, in common with every human being, is endowed" (43). Forten's own experience intensified the tension:

When I appeared at the dinner-table today, it seems that a *gentleman* took umbrage at sitting at the same table with one whose skin chanced to be "not colored like his own," and rose and left the table. Poor man! he feared contamination. But the charming part of the affair is that . . . such things do not wound me so deeply as of yore. But they create a bitterness of feeling which is far from desirable. "When, when will these outrages cease?" (133–34)

This plea for relief appears repeatedly in the diary. Forten tried to follow her teacher's advice and be charitable toward her enemies, and she found it "hard to go through life meeting contempt with contempt, hatred with hatred, fearing, with too good reason, to love and trust any one whose skin is white." Yet she found few whom she could trust. Even her fellow students, though "thoroughly kind and cordial" in the schoolroom, would, when she met them on the street, fear to recognize her or give "the most distant recognition possible" (47, 74).

Forten's need for achievement was strong. She cautioned herself against ambition, calling it "selfish"; yet she wrote that she was constantly asking herself, "What shall I do to be forever known?" (109–10). In the beginning of the very first entry she chided herself for having slept past sunrise. In another entry, written when she was "nearly twenty-one," she sought self-reform after expressing "sorrow shame and self-contempt" at the life she had "wasted . . . in idle day dreams" and her "want of energy perseverance and application" (121).

The relationship between this personal ambition and the problems of race become clarified in an entry in which she suggests that "colored persons" should refrain from some public actions "unless they can compare favorably with others" because they will not be judged as individuals but as examples of their race (76). There have been, she notes, blacks such as Phillis Wheatley, whose "character and genius afford striking proof of the falseness of the assertion . . . that hers is an inferior race" (55). Certainly, Forten's own grandfather, father, and uncle could be included among the list of blacks who had made distinguished accomplishments (12–29). However, Forten was all too aware that her task had been made difficult because of the restrictions of society. She might have access to great books, but she would not have the same "opportunities of studying those living, breathing, *human* books which [she considered] . . . the most profoundly interesting and human study" (129).

The statement above appears in the last entry of the first major section of the diary. Here the diary lapsed for almost two and a half years, until Forten was inspired by a fictional work written as "journal letters . . . addressed to an unknown friend."[14] She borrowed this pattern for her own work, addressing her "long neglected friend" by the initial "A." In August, 1862, she sought a position as a teacher of freed blacks in South Carolina. After failing to get an appointment from the Boston Port Royal Educational Commission, she applied to the Philadelphia Port Royal Relief Association and was accepted (32–33).

Forten's picture of the experiences and nature of blacks in the South is more like that in the diaries of Northern visitors such as Philip Fithian, who stressed the suffering of the slaves, than like that of Southern diarists, most of whom tended to portray slaves as contented and ignorant.[15] This part of Forten's work is comparable to Fanny Kemble's *Journal of a Residence on a Georgia Plantation,* written in a similar setting a quarter of a century earlier. Both women fought for the improvement of the physical and spiritual conditions of the blacks in the South.[16]

Forten's diary demonstrates that though the former slaves had an affection for America and sometimes for the plantations on which they had been slaves, few had any difficulty in choosing between their new freedom and their condition as slaves. In one entry (which also indicates her ability to transcribe the local dialect) Forten recorded the stories of some former slaves about attempts by their masters to lure them back into slavery. One told how his master had "tried to persuade him to go back with him, assuring him that the Yankees w'ld shoot them all when they came. 'Bery well sur,' he replied 'if I go wid you I be good as dead, so if I got to dead, I might's well dead here as anywhere. So I'll stay and wait for the Yankees.'" A second, "with a look and gesture of ineffable contempt," added that his former master had told him to put his wife and children on a boat and row them "'down to a certain pint, and den I c'ld come back if I chose.' Jus' as if I was gwine to be sich a goat" (161).

Forten told of one plantation owner who claimed "that she and her husband had devoted themselves to the good of their slaves, and lamented their ingratitude in all deserting her." In response a former slave disclosed "the jail on the place where chains and handcuffs" were and testified to the cruelty that had once been inflicted there (183). Interviewing black women who had had to watch helplessly as their children while still young were "dragged" from their mothers "to work in the cottonfields . . . cruelly beaten" or sold and sent away, Forten recorded examples of the mistreatment suffered by these former slaves (160).

Having obtained their freedom, some of the blacks at Port Royal enlisted in the Union Army so that they might preserve that liberty. Forten endorsed such action, believing that it would be better "to die in this sublime struggle for universal freedom, than live to see another generation of slavery," and she was obviously pleased to be able to note a report that showed that while the white soldiers were still contemptuous of the black troops, the former slaves had fought "nobly and bravely" (183, 192). Forten also emphasizes that black women too were capable of heroism. In one entry she tells of the courage displayed by two black girls who, having been taken away when the slaveholders fled before the Union occupation, "stole away at night, and traveled through woods and swamps, for two days without eating" until they finally were reunited with their parents (182).

Forten sought to teach her new pupils not only academic subjects, but also the ideas that might "inspire them with courage and ambition." For example, she told them the history of Toussaint L'Ouverture, "that they sh'ld know what one of their own color c'ld do for his race" (150). Forten entered her work hopefully; but, while she found her new pupils "eager to learn," some aspects of the situation, such as the presence of children "too young even for the alphabet," made her task difficult (147–48). Equally distressing to her was a special sort of loneliness. Even though the people were kind and grateful, she found no "congeniality," no one who could provide both the friendship and talents of her friends at home. Reminding herself to put away such "vain longings," she wrote: "Let the work to which I have solemnly pledged myself fill up my whole existence" (154).

Forten seems to have been caught between two worlds, one to which she was linked by education and cultural heritage, the other to which she was linked by the effects of prejudice and racial heritage. Nowhere in the diary is this dilemma clearer than in the following entry about David F. Thorpe, a student from Brown who had come to Port Royal as one of the superintendents (158, 266). After riding home with him one evening she wrote:

> I like Mr. T[horpe]. Report says that he more than likes me. But I *know* it is not so. Have never had the least reason to think it. Although he is very good and liberal, he is still an *American,* and w'ld never be so insane as to love one of the proscribed race. The rumor, like so many others, is absurd and without the shadow of a foundation. How strange it seemed riding to-night through the woods—often in such perfect darkness we could see nothing—how strange and wild! (207)

In the passage Forten said that Thorpe could not really love her, but she never said that she did not love him, and her tone suggests that his love should not have been "insane" any more than that her race should have been "proscribed." Again the diary shows the tension between Forten's ideal of a color-blind world and her awareness of current social realities.

At the end of July, 1863, Forten worked in a hospital, treating the wounded from an attack on Charleston, and then took a trip back to the North.[17] She returned to her work at Port Royal in October, 1863, but made few diary entries after that point.[18] She finally left Port Royal in May, 1864.

Chapter Five

Other Diaries of Situation

Most diaries, and all the diaries treated thus far, are diaries of situation. Diarists begin such works to record or to aid them in dealing with some special situations or incidents that have or are about to produce dislocations, whether major or minor, in their lives. In addition to the types already considered in this work, some of the common categories of situation diaries are spiritual journals and romance and courtship diaries. Examples in these categories that deserve to be listed among the best American diaries written in the late nineteenth century are those of Mollie Dorsey Sanford and Alice James.

Mollie Dorsey Sanford (1839–1915)

Despite elements that would suggest that Sanford's work is a travel diary, a close examination suggests that it is more appropriately classified as a romance and courtship diary. In her initial entry eighteen-year-old Mollie Dorsey writes the words "Hurrah! for Nebraska," but unlike Helen Carpenter's "Ho—for California," this happy shout is not hers, but rather that of an eight-year-old younger brother.[1] Dorsey's initial attitude was not joy in beginning a new life, but sadness in leaving an old one.[2] She feared that she was parting, "perhaps forever," from a classmate to whom she had "vowed 'eternal friendship,'" to "go among strangers" and leaving behind the church in which she had worshiped, taught, and begun her religious life to enter "a wild unsettled country" where there might not even be churches (1–3). The diary, she explained, was begun as a means to deal with such concerns.

Sanford wrote that she had not previously begun a diary because she thought her life "too monotonous to prove interesting," but that now that she was about to emigrate to "a new country" with "new scenes and new associations" she would have "experiences worth recording." However, this expectation of interesting experiences was not her only or even her principal reason for starting her diary; more important was the diary's potential as a substitute for "a confidant or bosom friend" after she had left behind those to whom she had been able to tell her "sorrows and joys" (1). The dislocation that prompts the diary is not really a physical dislocation but an emotional dislocation brought about by or emphasized by travel.

Even before she left her old home Sanford had begun writing about romance and courtship. The first entry after the introductory one centers about her rejection of a proposal of marriage, "I could 'stay and go into my own home tomorrow'—if I were ready, and he were the One"; but, having been "cured" by a previous relationship "from falling in love in a hurry," she left "heart whole and fancy free" (4). She gives an interesting description of the boat trip from St. Louis to Nebraska City, but even here she includes romance elements: a proposal from an elderly widower, the lament of another traveler whose parents had parted her from her lover, and the arrival of a bridal party.

The diary is full of interesting incidents that taken together give a picture of pioneer life. Sanford includes accounts of her brother's recovery from snakebite and her sister's religious conversion, along with her own work as a *"cook, general bottle washer, milk maid, school marm, seamstress, nurse . . . [and] Healer Magnetic"* (102). But the true heart of the diary is composed of those incidents that suggest the diarist's character (102). There is a special youthful vitality in Sanford's adventures, such as that in which she disguises herself in man's clothing to go in pursuit of a stray cow. Such behavior may have made her mother fear that Mollie was "losing all the dignity . . . [she] ever possessed," but the reader is more likely to be sympathetic to what "this wild life" developed in her (52–54). This exuberance with which she *"molli*fied" an inhospitable neighbor is most characteristic of the diary.

The early portion is full of such humorous anecdotes, which center about a young girl's flirtations. In one she tells of taking "a little ramble up into the town. Duly rigged in my spring bonnet and other finery, I expected to create a sensation. It was calm when I started, but before I ascended the hill, there came a gust of wind that sent my bonnet flying and flapped my garments about my form until I looked more like a liberty pole than the dashing belle I started to be." After adjusting her "ruffled plumage," Sanford went shopping, imagining that she had caught the attention of "a good looking black-eyed clerk." Only after "glancing into an 8 by 10 fly-bespecked looking glass" did she realize that her hat was askew, her hair undone, and the "whole costume out of gear" (16).

Behind these flirtations were more serious concerns about marriage.

In one entry Sanford writes, only partially in jest, that her father is building their log cabin "in the woods! miles and *miles* from any body" as a way to keep his daughters (19). Sanford's problem, though, was not the absence of suitors, but rather an uncertainty about which suitor to encourage. Early in the diary she records that she had been advised by the wife of one of the town's merchants "to set my cap for a Mr. By Sanford." After she had "admired him from across the street," she concluded "A good-looking enough fellow. *I'll see about it.*" Although she expresses her doubts about whether she would "*ever* love any man well enough to marry him or not" (20–23), these doubts are part of a pattern of using humor to hide concerns about finding the right husband.

It may be more than coincidence that at the same time that she declared that she had decided to encourage By Sanford's attentions, she wrote of receiving a letter from her former home telling of the marriage of her former lover: "Jim Hyatt is married!! There! that is as much as a distracted lover's threats amount to. When we parted two years ago, he swore he would '*kill* himself, that he would *never never* marry anyone else. He would *die* loving me alone.' . . . I wonder if he has written *her* as much poetry as he used to inscribe to *me*" (24–25).

In only a little more than a month after this entry Mollie notices that she has already started to call Mr. Sanford "mine." Three months after that her entries seem to indicate that she is certain about her choice: "Grandma has taken it into her dear old head that he [By Sanford] is my lover, and—I guess—well, my Journal, *I* could make a confession here—I believe he is myself. I knew today when he came, and I had not seen him for so long, that I cared for him" (40, 57). By her own admission she had matured significantly in these months. She had "had a nice time through the summer," but the coming of winter symbolizes for her that she is finally "ready for something else." On New Year's day, 1858, she records her engagement: "A happy greeting to you my Journal. Another leaf is turned in life's book, wherein shall be traced the deeds of good or ill." She has determined that the carefree days of youth are over and she will have "someone to worry over, some one to watch and wait for, someone to love and weep for" (61–62).

On February 13, 1860, she writes, "This is the last time I shall write in this journal as Mollie Dorsey." The next entry, her first as Mrs. Sanford, is written almost a week later, and it presents as comical the events of what must have been a very trying wedding day. Her husband, who had to travel to get the license, was late for the wedding: "Twelve! One! Two! Three o'clock came and no bridegroom," and by late afternoon she was tired of being taunted with tales of "harrowing incidents where the bridegrooms *never* came, and the brides ended their days in insane asylums." When, at last, By arrived, Mollie arranged to trick the guests by pretending to abandon the wedding before surprising them with a sudden ceremony. Mollie Sanford concluded her account of the wedding with her typical use of humor to cover a serious statement: "And we were married in the kitchen! Start not ye fairy brides, beneath your veils and orange blossoms, in some home where wealth and fashion congregate, *your* vows are no truer, your heart no happier than was this maiden's in the kitchen of a log cabin" (108–12).

The entries written after Mrs. Sanford's marriage are briefer and certainly less lighthearted than the earlier ones. Part of this change may be attributable to the effort required to travel to and set up a new home (127). Still, her earlier diary had thrived in the harsh conditions of her family's move to Nebraska. A better explanation may be that the diary's function as confidant had been assumed by her new husband. This hypothesis seems supported by the fact that the diary revives when her husband has to go away on business, leaving her to be "nearly frantic, not knowing what has become of him" in a "country full of cutthroats and robbers, ready to waylay the unprotected" (133–34). Her fears are not only for her husband, but for herself. In one incident the intrusion of a stranger makes her suddenly aware of "how unprotected I was, so far from home and friends. . . . I threw myself upon the floor and cried and cried until I was sick" (136). Even after her husband returned, his absences at work left her homesick.

Sanford used the diary to deal with such concerns. She composed two poems during this period. One focuses on how she loves her husband, but begins, "It was for him I left my happy home"; the other talks of an imaginary visit home "in spirit form" flying "swift as an uncaged bird" (141–44). Another entry, written on her first anniversary, is connected to her old home by its parallels to her wedding night when "the anxious waiting bride" remained confident of the bridegroom's arrival. In this entry Sanford's husband has also failed to come as expected; nevertheless, she "kept the kettle singing on the stove, the logs piled on the fire, and every few moments would peer out into the midnight darkness to catch the sound of his coming." At last he did arrive, having walked miles to be with her, and later with her husband "on the bed resting" she declared, "I [was] so happy I had to tell my journal" (152–53).

After this entry Sanford's diary keeping becomes even more sporadic. She managed only about one entry per month between that anniversary and September 25, 1861, when she again decided to "seek my Journal" to help her deal with her grief at the death of her newborn son (157). Another motive for her resumption of more regular entries was the Civil War. In the beginning of October, 1861, her husband received his commission as a lieutenant in the Colorado Volunteers. In this period the diary served to help Mrs. Sanford with her concerns about the dangers of battle. Fortunately, after some combat, Mr. Sanford returned and took the post of quartermaster. This tension resolved, Sanford's diary production again dropped off. The birth of a son in this period is another indication that the transition of roles that prompted the diary was complete. In her last entry, written after the birth of a daughter, Mrs. Sanford declares that "with my two little ones, I will have less time to journalize." She no longer needed a diary except as a "reminder of the past" (193).

Alice James (1848–1892)

At Alice James's own request her friend Katherine Loring arranged to have James's diary published. This edition, printed two years after its author's death, was limited to only four copies, one for each of her brothers. The diary first became public in 1934 in an imperfect edition that was included in a book by Anna Robeson Burr. Finally, in 1964 Leon Edel edited a complete scholarly edition.[3]

Alice James's diary shows her natural tendency to convert sensory impressions into artistic conceptions:[4] "Yesterday I was lying in a meadow at Hawkes farm absorbing like blotting-paper hayricks, hedges and trees composing themselves into a multitude of pictures . . . the foreground grey, with ghostly slants of sunshine, vanishing to reappear in the distance, so succulent, so smooth and so slow, so *from* all time and so *for* all time" (33–34). Yet while Alice longed to be a creative artist like her brother Henry, she feared to attempt to cultivate her talent lest she only increase her ability to perceive the beautiful and remain unable to effect beauty: "Imagine the joy and despair of it! the joy of seeing with the trained eye and the despair of *doing* it." Alice seemed to feel that it might be less painful to be dumb than to "ever find expression impotent to express!" (31).

Alice James's particular artistic tendencies seem to have been naturally suited to the diary form. Her creative vision did not emerge as a

developed whole but through a series of smaller developments: "I remind myself all the time of a coral insect building up my various reefs
by microscopic additions drawn from observation, or my inner consciousness, mostly" (109). Her diary grew from such small additions.
Ever since the end of 1886 she had kept a commonplace book for her
collection of quotations, and this book led to the development of her
diary (1). Even after May 31, 1889, when she began the true diary,
which she kept until her death on March 5, 1892, she still copied or
pasted into it quotations and news clippings.

In the beginning of the very first entry James claimed that her purpose in keeping a diary was twofold: to relieve her own melancholy
and to serve as an outlet for her creative inspiration: "I think that if I
get into the habit of writing a bit about what happens, or rather doesn't
happen, I may lose a little of the sense of loneliness and desolation that
abides with me. . . . and it may bring relief as an outlet to that geyser
of emotions sensations speculations and reflections which ferments perpetually within my poor old carcass for its sins" (25). The reference to
sins in this quotation is of importance because it is one of the more
obvious references to the diary's identity as a spiritual journal. During
most of her adult life, including the period of the diary, Alice James
was an invalid. She suffered constantly, but not until the last year of
her life, when she was diagnosed as having terminal cancer, were her
complaints clearly connected to a physical cause.

Though illness and death are major themes of the diary, James had
other concerns in her diary and in her life. For example, she paid a
good deal of attention to political issues, such as the struggle for Irish
independence. But even here her interests show some of the moral
concerns one finds in many spiritual journals. Her political concerns
centered about what is good.

James's diary shows her American democratic leanings in her distaste
for the English class system, especially the way the lower class "like a
cringing dog" seems so ready "to lick the hand that chastises." She
cites the example of her former landlady who "despised" the mayor of
her town "simply because he was one of her 'own kind.'" This landlady
could not accept the idea that a man who "had been a poor boy" could
be competent while, at the same time, insisting that "a stodgy fox-
hunting squire, in virtue of his having been always ignorant, idle and
selfish" was knowledgeable and honorable (157). James saw class distinction as a major impediment to the development of an "international
point of view" linking the British and the Americans. The British, she

complained, lacked the Americans' sense of "individual dignity" and felt "themselves to be primarily members of a class, and only secondarily human beings" (176).

Even though she admitted that she would "always be a bloated capitalist," James sympathized with the struggles of the working classes, and so could write of being delighted when those in power feared the public marches on May Day: "Could anything exhibit more beautifully the solidarity of the race than that by simply combining to walk thro' the streets on the same day, these starvelings should make Emperors, Kings, Presidents and millionaires tremble the world over!" (113).

James also had a sympathy for the victims of individual tragedy, such as a father who starved himself to death so that his children might eat and a young man who died of scarlet fever ten days after his wedding: "How cruel when pain and sorrow comes to young things,—they are so helpless; what can they do with it? What a rush of desire to go to them and wrap them in one's long accustomedness until the little bewildered soul has woven for itself some sort of casing" (73–74).

Constantly ill, Alice James was used to dealing with pain and suffering and lived with the possibility of death. Like Emily Dickinson, a poet whom she much admired and with whom she has sometimes been compared, James would attempt to experience death through her creative perception: "When death has come close how the emptiness seems palatable and to permeate the very atmosphere, making the sounds of life reverberate therein so loud" (185). James imagined her own death as the greatest scene in her life's drama: "I know I shall slump at the 11th hour, and it would complete it all so to watch the rags and tatters of one's Vanity in its insolent struggle with the Absolute, as the curtain rolls-down on this jocose humbuggery called Life!" Her only fear was that death would come while she was asleep and so prevent her from being "one of the audience." She declared that such an occurrence would be a "dreadful fraud! A creature who has been denied all the dramatic episodes might be allowed, I think, to assist at her own extinction" (135). Death here seems almost a religious experience, like the coming of the bridegroom in the Christian parable.

Alice James did not fear death but, rather, welcomed it as a release from the misery of the constant patter of illness and recovery, "the dreary snail-like climb up a little way so as to be able to run down again" (142). She wrote with ironic regret about one period of partial recovery: "There seems a faint hope that I may fizzle out, but the Monster *Rebound* which holds me in its remorseless clutch, I am sure will gather itself up for many another spurt" (135). Her words in such passages seem to prefigure not only Eliot's *Waste Land* but also, as the continuation of the above passage suggests with its black humor, some of the poems of Sylvia Plath. Like Plath, James had been approaching death since her youth, and yet she always was pulled back to life: "These doctors tell you that you will die, or *recover!* But you *don't* recover. I have been at these alterations since I was nineteen, and I am neither dead nor recovered" (142).

Several entries in the diary show that James considered suicide. In one she wrote: "I'll not use that word . . . [damn]⁵ which is denied with her other rights to *Women,* but I shall proclaim that any one who spends her life as an appendage to five cushions and three shawls is justified in committing the sloppiest kind of suicide at a moments notice" (81). However, she seems to have been more concerned with the right to control her life than with any real intention of ending it. She never rejected life, declaring in her diary "that of all the arts the art of living is the most exquisite and rewarding and that it is not brought to perfection by wallowing in disabilities." Nor did she see these rewards as beyond her reach: "The paralytic on his couch can have if he wants them wider experiences than Stanley slaughtering savages." The important thing, she concluded, was to use what one has rather than "waste then the sacred fire and wear away the tissues in vulgar pursuit of what others have and we have not" (146).

James's symptoms eventually grew so severe that beginning on December 31, 1890, she had to give up writing the diary in her own hand and, instead, began to dictate her entries to Kathleen Loring. One might expect that this presence of another at the moment of creation would affect the literary composition, especially in so private a form as a diary; however, there seems no significant change in the nature of the entries. Indeed, in the first part of the first entry that Alice dictated, she talked about Katherine and referred to her in the third person.

On May 27, 1891, James was diagnosed as having both a cardiac condition and terminal breast cancer. Four days later she wrote: "My aspirations may have been eccentric, but I cannot complain now, that they have not been brilliantly fulfilled. Ever since I have been ill I have longed for some palpable disease, no matter how conventionally dreadful a label it might have, but I was always driven to stagger back under the monstrous mass of subjective sensations" (206).

More than nine months before this diagnosis of cancer, James noted in the diary that her attitude toward death and immortality had changed. She had previously felt it necessary to conceive of death "as an entrance into spiritual existence . . . but now, altho' intellectually non-existence is more ungraspable and inconceivable than ever, all longings for fulfillment, all passion to achieve has died down within me and whether the great Mystery resolves itself into eternal Death or glorious Life, I contemplate either with equal serenity. It is that the long ceaseless strain and tension have worn out all aspiration save the one for Rest!" (131).

In her last entries Alice James reflected on the deaths of her father and her mother as part of a last consideration of the possibility and nature of something beyond death. Finally, she concluded that "the great Immortalities" lie not so much in conventional conceptions of the afterlife, but rather in "Love, Goodness and Truth" (217, 220–21). Her diary has assured a degree of immortality founded upon her concern for such values.

Chapter Six
Travel-Dominated Life Diaries

In dealing with the diaries of the middle and late nineteenth century, I have detected a group that defies precise classification. They demonstrate some of the features of length and complexity of life diaries, and to classify them as such would be convenient; however, to place them in that subgenre without qualification would ignore a special characteristic of these works. All are controlled by incidents of travel. In each instance, diary production was most often begun, resumed, increased, or terminated in response to periods of travel.

The diaries of Richard Henry Dana and Nathaniel Hawthorne are good examples of this type of diary because most of the entries were written during periods of travel. Other concerns seem to dominate some parts of these diaries; for example, Hawthorne's *Notebooks* did serve as literary notebooks, specifically recording ideas and information for later use in fictional works. But though these parts of the work are emphasized in most anthologies and critical studies, they actually comprise only a small portion of the whole. The other two diaries in this chapter were the work of diplomats George Mifflin Dallas and Benjamin Moran. Dallas preceded Charles Francis Adams as the American ambassador in Great Britain, and Benjamin Moran served as secretary to both men. These professional parallels provide opportunities for comparisons among these men and their diaries. However, in pursuing such comparisons, one must keep in mind that the works of Moran and Dallas are of a different form than that of Adams. Most diplomatic diaries are travel diaries, focusing on the special tension that comes from being in a new environment and usually coinciding with their authors' periods of diplomatic service. As we will see in the following chapter, Adams's record is a generalized life diary, and its production was not a response to his diplomatic role. The diaries of Moran and Dallas do go beyond the limits of the usual diary of situation, but they still focus on their authors' diplomatic roles and on other political or travel experiences related to those roles.

Richard Henry Dana, Jr. (1815–1882)

Dana prefaced his diary with "An Autobiographical Sketch" covering most of his life prior to his first formal diary entry. The sketch included the voyage to California that was the basis for *Two Years before the Mast* (1840), the novel which brought Dana such fame that it overshadowed all of his future efforts.[1]

Dana's introduction to his autobiographical sketch gives some hints of his reasons for resuming a diary, the desire to have "a correct account of all such [of] my acts, thoughts & feelings as I am willing to have known" (4). His sudden wish to preserve such an account may have come from a series of changes in his life that must inevitably have led him to reevaluate his future. Public reaction to *Two Years before the Mast,* published the year before the diary begins, had been so strong that he had to deal with an unexpected attention. In addition, he was married in August, 1840, and opened his law office in September.

The entry for December 17, 1841, begins: "With this day I begin my journal, writing down the events of each day, as they occur. All before this has been from memory." However, Dana's statement is somewhat misleading because he had kept a diary during the period covered by *Two Years before the Mast* and may have kept others.[2] Moreover, from the point at which he treats of his wedding, Dana's autobiographical sketch had already begun to assume a rough diary form, suggesting that he had resumed journalizing before the first formal entry (48).

It seems likely that Dana expected that all or part of his diary would become public. He read published diaries and had become an acquaintance of the diarist Dr. James Thacher.[3] Dana even prefaced the autobiographical section with an argument that no diarist could help but think about an audience or avoid subjectivity: "To be honest with myself and to any into whose hands this may come, I shall not profess to myself or pretend to them that this is a faithful transcription of the acts, feelings & thoughts of my life. . . . There will be no fiction & no dressing up of anything; but . . . there are thoughts & intents of the heart sometimes put forth in act which no man would be willing or need to open to all observers" (1:3–4).

That Dana strove for honesty is apparent from his inclusion of potentially embarrassing episodes, such as his encounter with prostitutes. According to the diary, Dana did not become involved sexually, but only sought to learn about their way of life and, in one instance, to reform them. Still, his own words suggest that such "adventures" seem to "possess" his mind (1:76–82, 119–22).

Another sign of the importance of such episodes in his life is that these entries were exceptionally lengthy. Dana's diary entries are not uniform. Many are short matter-of-fact notes with no thread connecting them. However, sometimes a compelling event would inspire a long and effective narrative. A picturesque village, an interesting law case, or the death of a friend would sometimes take control and produce both longer and more connected entries. Some of the more interesting of these unified sections include one series of entries written after the death of the painter Washington Allston and focusing on the disposition of *Belshazzar's Feast,* a painting left unfinished at Allston's death. Another important series tells of Dana's unsuccessful defense of Anthony Burns, a fugitive slave.

The major interest unifying the diary was travel. Dana wrote that at one point in his schooling he spent much of his time "pouring over maps & descriptive tables. . . . This pursuit fostered in me & perhaps in part sprang from, a strong desire to travel" (1:10). Dana went on numerous journeys, and about half of the diary consists of long travel sections. He spent a considerable amount of time on these trips; even so, they occupy a disproportionate amount of space in the diary. His trip to Europe in 1856 took only three months but occupies almost a third of a volume; his round-the-world tour in 1859–60 takes up the whole third volume. Readers will not regret the diary space lavished in these travel sections because, without the pressures of work, Dana could indulge his impulse to write. He often recorded detailed descriptions of the sights he saw, but he could be as effective even when he omitted details, as in the following excerpt from his account of Versailles:

I shall make no attempt to describe the palace, its halls, its ante-rooms, its sleeping chambers, its boudoirs, its closets, its rooms, its gold and precious stones, its curiously wrought wood and stone, and marble. Enough to say that you may let your fancy run riot in imagining generations of despotic monarchs, unrestrained, building pile after pile, gallery after gallery, and adding splendor to splendor, and luxury to luxury, and yet fall short of the reality. (2:811)

Dana left "with a sense of dreamy vision, not knowing of a surety, that [he] . . . had seen Versailles, but perhaps had been in a trance, or been looking into the glass of some potent conjurer" (2:813).

Dana's diary is full of encounters with some of the most interesting and important figures of his time, such as Henry Wadsworth Longfellow, George Ticknor, and William Cullen Bryant. They seem to have flitted almost casually into and out of Dana's life: Emerson taught him in school; Samuel Morse dropped by to talk about his telegraph; Horace Mann tried to convince him to revise *Two Years before the Mast;* John Brown gave him breakfast, Dana also gives the reader a feeling for the changes that were taking place in American society, such as technological and political developments. But he did not try to write an account of American history in the making; some major events were omitted or touched on only briefly because they didn't directly affect Dana's life. For example, the annexation of Texas is not mentioned and the Mexican War only becomes a subject for the diary when Dana records his discussions at a dinner with a general who had fought in it (2:342–44).

According to its editor, Dana's diary underwent a process of gradual deterioration that can be observed not only in the increasing fragmentation of entries, but even in the worsening handwriting in the manuscript.[4] Pressing business increasingly interfered with the diary, hastening its end. In the only entry for 1858 Dana wrote, "I omit writing in my journal almost entirely now—my duties are so constant" (2:832). Although he lived for twenty-three more years, with the exception of the diary of his world tour Dana managed only a few more entries.

Nathaniel Hawthorne (1804–1864)

At this writing there is no single edition that includes all the extant diaries and other serial records that Hawthorne kept during his lifetime. Most of his diary (over a million words) appears in three books: the *American Notebooks* (1835–53), the *English Notebooks* (1853–57), and the *French and Italian Notebooks* (1858–60).[5] The latter two volumes, constituting two-thirds of Hawthorne's record, invite classification as travel diaries.

Like Dana's, both the bulk of the whole as well as the longest sustained individual sections of Hawthorne's diaries are devoted to travel. The *English Notebooks* were written during Hawthorne's diplomatic posting as American Consul in Liverpool, England, beginning in 1853. The *French and Italian Notebooks* began with his departure for the Continent in January, 1858, and continued until June, 1859, shortly before his return home. Even the *American Notebooks* contains a large amount of travel-related material. Whole copybooks devoted to Hawthorne's trips, usually taken in the summer, comprise about one third of the *American Notebooks,* and if one includes as travel material such entries as those on Hawthorne's long residences at Brook Farm, the proportion of travel material is still more substantial.

Travel seems the primary motive for Hawthorne's first diary writing, although the earliest entries may be literary notes. Some of the early travel sections tell of trips with his friend Horatio Bridge whose diary, *Journal of an African Cruiser,* Hawthorne edited for publication.[6] Much of Hawthorne's earliest diary recorded periods of travel, and travel or actual travel often prompted a return to journalizing after a lapse. Moreover, travel experiences seem to have inspired him to sustain long and regular entries over extended periods.

In addition, however, two other types of material in Hawthorne's record are too distinct, too long, and too important to be dismissed. These consist of literary notebook entries, mostly undated, and portions of a true life diary, the longest section of which was written in 1842–1843.[7] These sections are usually considered important because they include a good deal of material bearing directly on Hawthorne's role as a professional writer. They also deserve attention because they suggest that his diary is more complex than it at first appears.

It is likely that, even when writing his earliest travel sections, Hawthorne recognized its beneficial effects on his creative writing. Of course, the mere practice of writing probably helped him to improve his style, but upon occasion these entries preserved and developed experiences and ideas that might be used in his fiction. Among the earliest entries are those preserved because they contained "the hint of a story" (*L,* 10). The idea might be expressed as a simple fact, image, event, or situation: "To make one's own reflection in a mirror the subject of a story" (*L,* 18), "a cannon transformed to church-bells" (*L,* 17), or "the life of a woman, who, by the old colony law, was condemned always to wear the letter A, sewed on her garment in token of her having committed adultery" (*A,* 254).[8]

Some of these ideas for stories were set down in sections of the notebooks reserved as a source for his writing; others appear with different diary material. An examination of such links between actual experiences and fictional works is useful in expanding our understanding of Hawthorne's perception of the relationship between life and fiction.

One especially memorable experience for Hawthorne was his participation "on July 9th, [1845 in] a search for the dead body of a drowned girl . . . a girl of education and refinement, but depressed and miserable for want of sympathy." Hawthorne described the search and the discovery in great detail, but he seemed particularly moved by the body itself: "They took her out of the water and deposited her under an oak-tree. . . . I never saw nor imagined a spectacle of such perfect horror. The rigidity above spoken of was dreadful to behold. . . . it is impossible to express the effect of it; it seemed that she would keep the same posture in the grave" (A, 261–65). This entry provided the idea and language for a major scene in *The Blithedale Romance.*[9]

Another excerpt, in which Hawthorne developed the idea for his romance "Ethan Brand," suggests an attraction and a potential danger of diary keeping, a search into the dark recesses of the soul:

"The search of an investigator for the Unpardonable Sin;—he at last finds it in his own heart and practice. . . .

The Unpardonable Sin might consist of a want of love and reverence for the Human Soul; in consequence of which the investigator pried into its dark depths not with the hope or purpose of making it better, but from a cold philosophical curiosity,—content that it should be wicked in whatever kind or degree, and only desiring to study it out. Would not this, in other words, be the separation of the intellect from the heart?" (A, 251)

This entry was not the first related to "Ethan Brand." In another passage, a portion of a long entry written in a section of travel diary, Hawthorne described a walk at night during which he found a lime kiln:

There are several of these lime kilns in the vicinity; they are built circular with stones, like a round tower, eighteen or twenty feet high having a hillock heaped around a considerable of their circumference, so that the marble may be brought and thrown in by cart loads at the top. At the bottom there is a door-way large enough to admit a man in a stooping posture. (A, 144)

With little modification the diary language appears in Hawthorne's romance:

It was a rude tower-like structure about twenty feet high heavily built of rough stones, and with a hillock of earth heaped about the larger part of its circumference; so that the blocks and fragments of marble might be drawn by cart-loads, and thrown in at the top. There was an opening at the bottom of the tower, like an oven mouth, but large enough to admit a man in a stooping posture.[10]

Hawthorne used his diary as part of his search for "remarkable characters," and among those he discussed at length in his diaries was a "disagreeable"-looking man dressed in dirty clothes and lacking half an arm and toes of one foot, who offers more of interest than the story of his lost limbs. "'My study is man,' said he. And looking at me 'I do not know your name,' said he, 'but there is something of the hawk-eye about you too.' This man was formerly a lawyer in good practice, but taking to drinking, was reduced to this lowest state. . . . 'you and I' said the squire, alluding to their respective troubles and sicknesses 'would have died long ago if we had not the courage ot live.' [He gave] vent to much practical philosophy and just observation on the ways of men mingled with rather more assumption of literature and cultivation, than belonged to the present condition of his mind" (*A*, 90–93). Such entries helped the writer to develop his skills in characterization.

It may have been a result of his attempt to develop character studies in his diary that Hawthorne reached some of his conclusions about the tendency of most people to disguise their true natures in their attempts to hide the darker sides of their characters. After one of the longest pieces in the diary, a 1400-word character study of "an old man at the railroad station-house at Salem," Hawthorne still complained that he felt unable to depict his subject adequately because "it requires a very delicate pencil to depict a portrait that has so much of the negative in it." Hawthorne wished that he could "follow him home, and see his domestic life" and thus not be limited to "his outward image, as shown to the world" (*A*, 222–26).

Diary keeping taught Hawthorne other lessons about the limits of art:

How narrow, scant and meagre, is this record of observation, compared with the immensity that was to be observed . . . How shallow scanty a stream of thought too,—of distinct and expressed thought—compared with the tide of dim emotions, ideas, associations, which were flowing through the haunted regions of imagination, intellect and sentiment. . . . When we see how little we can express, it is a wonder that any man takes up a pen a second time. (A, 250)

Hawthorne found that his best efforts to imitate the world in his art were flawed, as was all human art. "Man's finest workmanship, the closer you observe it, the more imperfections it shows:—as, in a piece of polished steel, a microscope will discover a rough surface.—whereas, what may look coarse and rough in nature's workmanship, will show an infinitely minute perfection, the closer you look into it" (L, 46). However, this discovery did not cause Hawthorne to abandon his hope to become an artist. Rather, as the diary illustrates, he sought to discover nature's secrets. He came to the conclusion that "the reason of the minute superiority in Nature's workmanship over man's, is that the former works from the innermost germ, while the latter works merely superficially" (L, 47). The application of this realization is apparent in Hawthorne's fiction, which develops minutely detailed symbols and images and then replicates them in increasingly larger patterns until they become apparent in the overall structures and broadest themes of his works.

Hawthorne's diary also grew in complexity from a record of particular details to a full life dairy. This transformation seems most obvious in a section kept after his marriage to Sophia Peabody in 1842. The Hawthornes moved to Concord and took up residence in "the Old Manse." This section, one of the longest and best in the diary, gives a detailed picture of Hawthorne's new world, the house, its furnishings, and its surroundings. He wrote of the "ten-foot square apartment" where he did his writing, the "sluggish stream" where he went to swim and fish, the garden where he planted his beans and squash, and the woods and fields (including those around Walden Pond) in which he walked (A, 315).

Hawthorne repeatedly compared his existence to Adam's in paradise, but unlike Adam, Hawthorne had visitors. Among the notables who came to the "sacred precincts" of his "paradise" to feast on "nectar and ambrosia" and listen "to the music of the spheres" were "Mr. [Ralph Waldo] Emerson . . . with a gnome yclept Ellery Channing," Henry Thoreau, and Margaret Fuller (A, 316–40). Had these individuals proved unimportant in American culture they would live in the pages of Hawthorne's diary. However, since they are now recognized as some of the major figures of the period, Hawthorne's portraits seem especially valuable. Consider, for example, a small fraction of Hawthorne's description of Thoreau:

> Mr. Thorow dined with us yesterday. He is a singular character—a young man with much of wild original nature still remaining in him; and so far as he is sophisticated, it is in a way and method of his own. He is ugly as sin, long nosed and queer-mouthed, and with uncouth and somewhat rustic, although courteous manners corresponding well to such an exterior. But his ugliness is of an honest and agreeable fashion, and becomes him much better than beauty. (*A*, 353–54)

Just as Thoreau's "ugliness" is "better than beauty" so everything in this world seemed transformed for the new husband; all of it offered lessons about nature and the human spirit. A period of rain inspired several pages of diary about "the infinity of raindrops [because of which] the whole landscape, grass trees and house, has a completely watersoaked aspect, as if the earth were wet through." Yet even "this somber weather, when ordinary mortals forget that there ever was any golden sunshine, or will ever be hereafter," was brightened by his wife, who seemed "absolutely to radiate it from her heart and mind" (*A*, 348–49).

For a month Hawthorne kept long and regular entries and then began to neglect the diary. At the end of one of the lapses he offered an explanation of his failure to continue this life diary: "I am sorry that our journal has fallen so into neglect; but unless my naughty little wife will take the matter in hand, I see no chance of amendment. All my scribbling propensities will be far more gratified in writing nonsense for the press; so that any gratuitous labor of the pen becomes peculiarly distasteful" (*A*, 363). This statement suggests that the prevalence of the travel diary material in Hawthorne's record resulted from different motives than that which inspired most travel diaries. Instead of developing in response to the tensions and interests of new situations, Hawthorne's travel diaries may have been produced and maintained because during such periods the author was released from the pressure, often self-imposed, to concentrate his writing on works for publication.

If this explanation is accurate, the rest of his diary, though mostly written during travel periods, is not truly a travel diary but really a variation of life diary. The test of this hypothesis requires a search of the later travel sections for the complexities and multiple motives of the life diary.

The longest of Hawthorne's diaries is the *English Notebooks*. Its first entry is that for August 4, 1853, a little over two weeks after he arrived in England to assume his post as American Consul in Liverpool. Hawthorne's experiences in the consulate had much in common with those that we will see in the London embassy diaries of Dallas, Moran, and Adams. He was besieged by "the most rascally set of sailors that were ever seen—dirty, desperate, and altogether pirate like in aspect," women "of no decided virtue," all asking for aid (*E*, 3–4). He complained that, "all penniless Americans, or pretenders to Americanism, look upon me as their banker; and I could ruin myself, any week, if I had not laid down a rule to consider every applicant for assistance an impostor, until he proves himself a true and responsible man" (*E*, 33).

The diary is not a political diary; only a small portion of it was devoted to comments on Hawthorne's work as a consul. Another sign of the nature of his record as a travel diary is that a persistent common subject is the differences between England and the United States. In the first entry Hawthorne began to express such differences, considering the "tall, dismal, smoke-blackened, ugly brick warehouse" that he sees from the consulate window as "Uglier than any building I ever saw in America" (*E*, 3). Even after a long stay in England some of this prejudice remained. In one entry Hawthorne even suggests that "the American clouds are more picturesque than those of Great Britain" (*E*, 519). Yet his feelings were mixed. He also wrote, "How misty is England! I have spent four years in a gray gloom. And yet it suits me pretty well" (*E*, 444). And in the last entry written in England Hawthorne noted that he had "been so long in England that it . . . [seemed] a cold and shivery thing to go anywhere else" (*E*, 621). Even years later, looking back, he remembered his conflicting impressions and wrote that while he "seldom came into personal relations with an Englishman without beginning to like him . . . [and] never stood in an English crowd without being conscious of hereditary sympathies," he was moved by such characteristics as the tendency of the English to "think so loftily of themselves, and so contemptuously of everyone else" that he often used his journal for "jotting down the little acrimonies of the moment."[11]

Part of Hawthorne's reaction to the English may be ascribed to a defensive patriotism. Visiting the British Museum with its "numberless treasures beyond all price," including the "letters of statesmen and warriors, of all nations and several centuries back," he insisted that "none of these were so illustrious as that of Washington, nor more so than Franklin's whom American gave to the world in her non-age" (*E*, 612).

One source of Hawthorne's ambivalence may have been internal rather than external: his perception of the relationship between England and his own ancestral past. At one point in the diary he noted his "wish to ascertain the place, in England, whence the family emigrated" (*E*, 383–84). After a trip to the English Boston in Lincolnshire, the origin of many of the early settlers, he wrote: "The crooked streets and narrow lanes reminded me much of the North End of American Boston—Hanover street and Ann street as I remember that region in my early days. It is singular what a home-feeling and sense of kindred, this connection of our new England metropolis gives me and how reluctant I am to leave the old town on that account" (*E*, 479).

From his earliest "street-rambles" Hawthorne was fascinated by the "life and domestic occupation in the streets . . . in all these meaner quarters of the city—nursing of babies, sewing and knitting, sometimes even reading," and suggested that "in a drama of low life, the street might fairly and truly be the one scene where everything should take place—courtship, quarrels, plot, and counter-plot." However, while he might describe the "roar of the city" as "that great Lullaby" (*E*, 601), more often he would focus on the suffering that he saw there: people submitting "to starvation meekly patiently" or enduring life in the workhouse, "women or girls in the streets picking up fresh horse-dung with their hands," a hospital so crowded that the staff "were compelled to lay some of the patients on the floor" (*E*, 104, 105, 110, 254–55). At one point he determined to "study this English street-life more and think of it more deeply" (*E*, 17). Hawthorne planned to write a novel based on his residence in England, but never did so. However, many of the experiences recorded in the *English Notebooks* became the basis for a series of sketches published under the title *Our Old Home*.

Not all of his entries suggest his powers of sympathy for the English, and the reader of the diary may conclude that Hawthorne's claim that he liked most Englishmen was exaggerated; indeed, if the term *Englishmen* was intended to include English women, the claim is clearly a false one. Some of the passages in the *English Notebooks* make him appear a misogynist. In one entry he wrote, "The women of England are capable of being more atrociously ugly than any other human beings; and I have not yet seen one whom we should distinguish as beautiful in America." Such women had, he complained, "an awful ponderosity of frame. You think of them composed of sirloins and with broad and thick steaks in their immense rears. . . . nothing of the gossamer about them; they are elephantine" (E, 27–28). In a later entry he called them so "gross and hideous" that "a man would be justified in murdering them—taking a sharp knife and cutting away their mountainous flesh, until he had brought them into reasonable shape, as a sculptor seeks for the beautiful form of a woman in a shapeless block of marble" (E, 88). American women did not fare much better. Comparing English matrons to his own countrywomen, Hawthorne complained that the choice was "between a greasy animal and an anxious skeleton."[12]

Hawthorne was often affected by the grandeur created for the English nobles, but he saw aristocracy as a frequent obstacle to true nobility of mind. Visiting Westminster Abbey, he was not as impressed by the faded "splendor of those tombs and monuments" of the dead royalty as by those of great figures such as Addison. And, he noted, "the monuments of the persons we remember best, either in history or literature" are not in the abbey because "rank has been the general passport to admission here" (E, 618). He was particularly upset by the way many of his fellow Americans were so willing to reject their nation's egalitarian principles by fawning over titled aristocrats: "There is something about royalty that turns the Republican Brain" (E, 118). Yet Hawthorne found some value in the sense of order and stability in British society. "It is," he wrote, "rather wearisome, to an American, to think of a place where no change comes for centuries, and where a peasant does but step into his father's shoes, and lead just his father's life, going in and out over the old threshold, and finally being buried close by his father's grave, time without end; and yet it is rather pleasant to know that such things are."[13]

Hawthorne seems to have been most favorably disposed toward British life when describing rural scenes: "I question whether any part of the world looks so beautiful as England—this part of England at least on a fine summer morning. It makes one think the more cheerfully of human life to see such a bright universal verdure; such sweet rural peace, flower border cottages; not cottages of gentility, but real dwellings of the rural poor" (E, 127).

Much of Hawthorne's *English Notebooks* is basically a record of trips to such tourist locations as Stratford-on-Avon, Blenheim Castle, and the lake country, and the diary is full of long descriptions of castles, gardens, and churches. Writing about his trips to London he not only included accounts of visits to such popular tourist spots as Westminster Abbey, the Houses of Parliament, and the Tower of London, but also descriptions of the "tumblers, hand-organists, puppet-showmen, musicians, Highland bag-pipers, and all such vagrant mirthmakers . . . numerous on the streets" (*E*, 215–18, 225).

One frequent companion on these trips was the Englishman Henry Arthur Bright, who later kept a diary of his own travels in America.[14] After one of his trips with Bright, a "delightful tour" of Wales, Hawthorne emphasized the importance of making an immediate record of experiences before "it is too late to describe [them]; the sharpness of the first impression being gone—" even though "something of the sentiment" might be recalled later (*E*, 66). However, as Hawthorne noted, even a prompt record might not be adequate. Sometimes the attempt proved futile, the "wonderful adornment" something "to be seen and marveled at, not written about" (*E*, 598). His main concern about his diary was not its failure to record such impressions, but rather that it did not immediately result in the novel he hoped to glean from his experience in England.[15] He condemned himself for "leading an idle life," while still hoping that his efforts might "not be quite thrown away; as I see some things, and think many thoughts" (*E*, 618). Many ideas, scenes, and characters in the notebooks are extensive and well suited for use in some fiction. Some appear in *Our Old Home*, but only a few made so strong an impression that they found their way into Hawthorne's fiction. One of these was the "bloody footprint" at Smithell's Hall that, according to legend, was made by a martyr during the reign of "Blood Mary." This legend not only appears twice in the *English Notebooks* (*E*, 106, 194–95), but also in *Grimshaw, The Ancestral Footstep*, and *Septimius Felton* (*E*, 635n).

Another experience mentioned in the notebooks that figures prominently in both *Our Old Home* and Hawthorne's fiction is a strongly anti-Semitic description of the brother of David Salomons, first Jewish Lord Mayor of London:

There sat the very Jew of Jews; the distilled essence of all the Jews that have . . . been born since Jacob's time; he was Judas Iscariot; he was the Wandering Jew; he was the worst, and at the same time the truest type of his race. . . . I never beheld anything so ugly and disagreeable, and preposterous and laughable, as the outline of his profile; it was so hideously Jewish, and so cruel so keen; and he had such an immense beard that you could see no trace of a mouth, until he opened it to speak or eat his dinner,—and then, indeed, you were aware of a cave, in this density of beard. And yet his manners and aspect, in spite of all, were those of a man of the world, and a gentleman. . . . I rejoiced exceedingly in this Shylock, this Iscariot; for the sight of him justified me in the repugnance I have always felt for this race. (*E, 321*)

Hawthorne made anti-Semitic statements elsewhere in his writings, but none so extreme. In the absence of any action on the man's part to prompt this outburst, one may wonder why Hawthorne expressed such obvious prejudice at this point.[16] Fortunately, for our understanding of Hawthorne and his diary, the work does contain a possible explanation. While in no way excusing Hawthorne's anti-Semitic remarks, other material in the diary suggests that they may have been a convenient weapon for an attack with a far different motive.

Immediately preceding this attack Hawthorne had written a long description of a lady whose appearance was so striking that he later used it as the basis for that of Miriam, one of the central characters in his novel *The Marble Faun*:

My eyes were drawn to a young lady who sat nearly opposite me, across the table. She was dark, and yet not dark, but rather seemed to be of pure white marble, yet not white but of the purest and finest complexion. . . . Her hair was a wonderful deep raven black, black as night, black as death . . . but it was hair never to be painted, nor described—wonderful hair, Jewish hair. Her nose had a beautiful outline, though I could see that it was Jewish too; and that all her features were so fine that sculpture seemed a despicable art beside her; and certainly my pen is good for nothing. . . . and looking at her I saw what were the wives of the old patriarchs, in their maiden or early married days—what Rachel was, when Jacob wood her seven years, and seven years more—what Judith was; for womanly as she looked, I doubt not she could have slain a man, in a good cause—what Bathsheba was; only she seemed to have no sin in her—perhaps what Eve was although one could hardly think her weak enough to eat the apple. (*E, 321*)

Not only was this woman the prototype for Hawthorne's Miriam, whose "Jewish hair" had a "dark glory such as crowns no Christian maiden's head,"[17] but she is also described in ways that suggest Hawthorne's other two memorable heroines: Hester Prynne of *The Scarlet Letter* and Zenobia of *The Blithedale Romance*. Each of these Dark Ladies possesses the same sort of beauty.[18]

In reading about any of these heroines one can recognize a sensual power that Hawthorne may have found both attractive and frightening. The following lines at the end of Hawthorne's description of the Jewish beauty in the Notebooks encourages the same conclusion: "I never should have thought of touching her, nor desired to touch her . . . I felt a sort of repugnance, simultaneous with my perception that she was an admirable creature" (*E*, 321).

Hawthorne's attempt to disclaim desire is followed in the diary by his description of the mayor's brother, and that description is followed by the revelation that "the beautiful Jewess" was this man's wife (*E*, 321). Retelling this incident in *Our Old Home*, Hawthorne removed all references to the Jewishness of the individuals and downplayed his own personal reactions. However, that version contains some material further suggesting that Hawthorne's reaction to the incident reveals his inner conflict about his own sexuality. Especially telling is his symbolic identification of the couple as "Bluebeard and a new wife (the loveliest of the series, but already with a mysterious gloom overshadowing her fair young brow) traveling on their honeymoon."[19]

Many other incidents in the diary are important to understanding Hawthorne's personality. Among the most notable is the persistence of a dream that Hawthorne had had for "twenty or thirty years" and that not only continued to recur, but also repeatedly invaded his waking life, giving him "a feeling of shame and depression" whenever he recalled it. In the dream he would find himself back at school or college, depressed by a conviction that "I have been there unconscionably long, and have quite failed to make such progress in life as my contemporaries have." Hawthorne attributed the dream to "that heavy seclusion in which I shut myself up, for twelve years after college, when everybody moved onward and left me behind." Hawthorne was especially disturbed that he could not account for its persistence: "How strange that it should come now when I may call myself famous and prosperous!—when I am happy, too!—still that same dream of life hopelessly a failure!" (*E*, 98).

Hawthorne's simultaneous desire for and insecurity about his own fame is one of the persistent themes in the notebooks. One can sense this desire for fame in his repeated visits to Westminster Abbey and his comments about how the abbey made him feel, "not how many great, wise, witty, and bright men there are—but how very few in any age, and how small a harvest of them for all the ages" (*E*, 235). Hawthorne hoped to be considered such a great man, but he seems to have been ill at ease when receiving praise either from those he respected such as Leigh Hunt or the Brownings or from those he considered less worthy of his respect such as the English author Martin Tupper, whom he called an "absurd little man (*E*, 255, 381–83, 393).

Hawthorne was often uncomfortable in his role as a celebrity. He complained that at one party "a good many persons sought the felicity of knowing me, and had little or nothing to say when that honor or happiness was conferred on them." It was, he felt, "wrong and ill-mannered in people to ask for an introduction, unless they . . . [were] prepared to make talk" because it would force him "on the spur of the moment, to concoct a conversable substance out of thin air, perhaps for the twentieth time that evening" (*E*, 367). He seems to have sympathized with Tennyson's attempt to "defend" himself from the impositions of the public by "ignoring them altogether" (*E*, 553).

Hawthorne continued as consul at Liverpool for four years, and then was replaced by an appointee of the new president, James Buchanan. The diary contains no mention of his resignation, but the last entry in the *English Notebooks* suggests that Hawthorne was ready to return to private life. "Ushered . . . with great courtesy into the waiting-room" of the American embassy where he had gone to get a passport for travel to the Continent, Hawthorne remarked, "This is the deference which an American servant of the public finds it expedient to show his sovereigns. Thank heaven I am a sovereign again, and no longer a servant" (*E*, 620).

Though in his *English Notebooks* Hawthorne often focused on comparisons between England and America, in that portion of his diary published as the *French and Italian Notebooks* he sometimes questioned whether the experiences of his travels were sufficiently distinct from familiar ones to allow him to preserve his sense of contrast; he tended to focus less on the difficulty of depicting an external scene and more on preserving the subjective sense of wonder. Commenting on the Louvre's collection of sketches by Raphael, da Vinci, Michelangelo, Rubens, and Rembrandt, Hawthorne saw that these "rude off-hand sketches" may have given their creators a "satisfaction which they never felt again in the same work . . . [even] after they had done their best" because these were "the earliest dawnings of their great pictures, [created] when they had the glory of their pristine idea directly before the mind's eye—that idea which inevitably became overlaid with their own handling of it, in the finished painting" (*F*, 23). The very diary in which Hawthorne recorded this observation was used in the same manner that these artists had used their sketches, as an attempt to capture a fleeting idea, to make "a symbol . . . perceptible to mortal senses."[20]

Unfortunately, the keeping of a diary of exploration or travel presents special obstacles to such realization of artistic symbols even as it makes them possible. As Hawthorne found, an important perception may occur at an inconvenient place and time. Another obstacle might be the very magnitude and frequency of the beauties. In one passage he wrote: "I soon grew so weary of admirable things that I could neither enjoy nor understand them," and he compared this satiation of his "receptive faculty" with "having dainties forced down the throat long after the appetite was satiated" (*F,* 49). Walking along a street in Rome, Hawthorne "came unawares to the Basilica of Santa Maria Maggiore, on the summit of the Esquiline hill . . . [and] entered it without knowing what church it was" (*F,* 65). Of just one chapel in it he remarked, "I found it most elaborately magnificent—more so I think, than any other church, or part of a church, that I was ever in. But one magnificence dazzles out another, and makes itself the brightest conceivable for the moment." Then that moment passed, leaving Hawthorne to express his disappointment at having "to leave this chapel and church without being able to say one thing that may reflect a portion of their beauty or the feeling which they excite" (*F,* 65–66). And if this frustration at an unrealized record was not sufficient, on his return from the church Hawthorne found the experience repeated. Wandering into a piazza he saw "a fountain, an obelisk, and two naked statues. . . . The obelisk was, as the inscription said, a relic of Egypt; the basin of the fountain was an immense bowl of oriental granite . . . the statues were colossal, two beautiful young men, each holding a fiery steed. On the pedestal of one was the inscription—OPUS PHIDIAE; on the other—OPUS PRAXITILIS. What a city this is where one may stumble by mere chance—at a street corner, as it were—on the works of two such sculptors" (*F,* 66–67).

Sometimes the real experience of some famous sight fell far short of the idealized one that the diarist had envisioned in his imagination. After visiting the Vatican Hawthorne wrote:

I have come—I think, finally—to the conclusion that there was a better St. Peter's in my mind, before I came to Rome, than the real one turns out to be—without definite outline, it is true, and with but misty architecture, dim, and gray, and vast, with an interminable perspective, and a dome like the cloudy firmament, and a space beneath for the soul to feel its immensity, or the personal man his littleness. This little piece of cabinet-work, big as it strives to be, cannot make up for what I have lost. (*F,* 136)

Hawthorne went to the Continent to see such art and architecture, and his attempts to record them fill many of the pages of his notebooks;

yet his most memorable experiences came in forms he had not expected. Visiting a Capuchin church in Rome, he saw a sight that he would "never forget." It was not any of the sights that he had come to view, but rather the body of a dead monk. Seeing "some blood oozing from . . . [the] nostrils" of the corpse, Hawthorne drew upon folk superstitions to speculate: "Perhaps his murderer . . . had just then come into the church and drawn nigh the bier" (F, 81). This episode became an important scene in *The Marble Faun*.

As these examples suggest, even when an aesthetic experience went unrealized, the diarist's emotional response might be, and the pattern of surprise could be an important rhetorical device. For example, in one entry Hawthorne described entering a building whose exterior had "no pretensions to beauty or majesty, or architectural merit of any kind," and yet had an interior whose "space is so lofty, broad and airy, that the soul forthwith swells out, and magnifies itself, for the sake of filling it" (F, 89). It was the diarist's awe rather than the beauty itself that had become the real subject for the diary.

There are other subjects in the *French and Italian Notebooks* besides such tourists' accounts of art, architecture, and scenery. But even most of the people Hawthorne saw seem almost to be portraits or scenery rather than characters. Among the exceptions are a few English and American travelers or expatriates, such as the Brownings, Franklin Pierce, and William Cullen Bryant. One of the most plausible explanations for this situation is the language barrier, but another is Hawthorne's basic distrust of foreign cultures: "It is very disheartening not to be able to place the slightest reliance in the integrity of the people we are to deal with; not to believe in any connection between their words and their purposes; to know that they are telling you lies, while you are not in a position to catch hold of the lie and hold it up in their faces" (F, 227). Hawthorne claimed that "No place ever took so strong a hold on my being as Rome, nor ever seemed so close to me and so strangely familiar. I seem to know it better than my birthplace, and to have known it longer" (F, 524). Yet, after the year and a half of travel covered in the *French and Italian Notebooks*, Hawthorne does not appear to have learned much about the French or Italian people.

He returned to England on June 22, 1859, and embarked for the United States a few weeks later. His return home ended his travels and the diary that focused on travel.

George Mifflin Dallas (1792–1864)

Both of the published portions of Dallas's diary cover diplomatic missions.[21] The first section treats his ministry to Russia from his arrival on July 29, 1837, until his departure on July 24, 1839. The second treats his service as ambassador to the Court of St. James, beginning with his attendance at the opening of Parliament, December 3, 1857, and ending May 1, 1861, when he received a note that his successor, Charles Francis Adams, had embarked for England.[22]

Although part of a longer and more complex record, the diplomatic sections of the diary (especially those written in Russia) seem essentially individual diaries of incident. These "diplomatic travel diaries" have very distinct termini that seem intended to set them apart from any account of earlier or later events. The Russian diary begins with a prefatory paragraph about the two days on ship prior to docking and ends with the insertion of a poem appropriately entitled "Home's Before Us," announcing that although Europe has many "bright attractions," it cannot compete with his native land (213–14). In the case of the British diaries, the first entry's account of the opening of Parliament seems symbolic of Dallas's new position, and his speculation on the Civil War about to begin signals his return home. There is further evidence in the next to last entry in which Dallas announces his intent to resume the diary after a month's lapse in order "to preserve the features of my few days remaining in this great country, which, while commanding my highest admiration, I find, after five years of trial, I do not and cannot like" (442). As in leaving Russia, Dallas was going home from travels in a foreign land.

Dallas obviously read travel literature and had his own idea of the functions and limits of the form. In one entry he excused, even while criticizing, the errors and exaggerations in one book on travel in Russia. The diary is full of detailed descriptions of the wonders he saw in Europe. Describing an impressive array of receptions, balls, masquerades, carnivals, and ceremonies, Dallas creates a wondrous world. However, this world is not without its drawbacks. He demonstrates that even in the first half of the nineteenth century one might encounter spies and secret police. "Your principal household servants," wrote Dallas, "are represented to be secret agents of this body, who will affect ignorance of your language and great personal fidelity, and yet be knowing and dextrous enough to understand and communicate everything to their employers." In an entry early in the Russian diary Dallas was distressed to find that a letter in which his wife had written too freely about her reactions "to the Imperial family and to Russian society in general" was mysteriously missing. After much suspicion and active search the letter was fortunately found "sticking to the under surface of the table" (29–30). Even the grandeur of the court could not hide the fear and suspicion which lay behind such measures. When the Winter Palace burned, there was an almost immediate concern about revolution. "In despotic governments," Dallas wrote, "fears of conspiracy and change are almost always afloat. The agents of the police keep these fears alive as necessary to their own importance" (45).

Although a Jacksonian Democrat, Dallas clearly did not look with favor on the prospect of a Russian Revolution. He considered the present emperor best "fitted for Russia in her actual condition, and . . . [most] capable of pushing her onward toward European ascendancy" (48). Dallas draws a highly favorable portrait of the emperor, reporting his statement that "human life is infinitely more valuable than human treasure" (48).

Although Dallas devoted most of the diary to the description of external events and observations, his character and personal concerns can be seen through close reading. At the time of his mission to Russia he had already held several important positions, including that of United States senator, and his family was becoming one of the most important in Philadelphia; nevertheless, Dallas was less secure in his wealth and social position than were American ambassador-diarists Gouverneur Morris and John Quincy Adams.[23] Although this insecurity may have been to some extent obviated by his possession of an official title, the friendly treatment he received from members of the royal family, and his political heritage as an American democrat, Dallas in the diary betrays an obvious concern about the difficulties he faced in competing for prominence in the society of the imperial court. In one entry he expresses his belief that because Americans "had no titles, nobility, or European distinction or wealth," he can make no true friendships in Russian society (154).

Dallas seems to have had an easier time dealing with his uneasiness about social position than he did about his relatively limited wealth. When he recorded his admiration for the splendid attire and furnishings of those at court, he frequently added criticism or qualification. Going to a "*soirée* at . . . one of the handsomest and most richly-furnished houses in St. Petersburg," he made a point to record that "the magic of wealth" that created this palace came as the result of a marriage to a woman who was "the personification of an indented toad stool," and that it had made a count of a man who is not only "short mean, and insignificant in appearance," but who came to Russia "as a French hairdresser" (34–35).

Of his own residence, Dallas explained that he had found it necessary "to unite taste with as much simplicity as the subject-matter would admit" because any attempt at "vying, even remotely, with the gorgeous extravagance exhibited by the principal members of the circle in which as a national representative I necessarily must move in this capital . . . would be equally out of character, in bad taste, and utterly futile" (34). It was probably easier for Dallas to accept the vast discrepancy between his wealth and position and that of the emperor and his court, than that between his and that of other ambassadors. Attending a royal function, Dallas devalued the expensive and ornate attire of the other ambassadors' wives and praised his own wife's "white satin gown flounced with tulle, and a head-dress of a few flowers . . . unadorned by a single jewel of any sort" as "exceedingly modest, particularly suited to an American lady, and, withal, really much the prettiest" (141–42).

It was not only the grandeur of the court that attracted Dallas's attention. Declaring that "the commonest and most constantly recurring appearances are singular to our eye and taste" and that "the streets afford at every step something for comment," Dallas shows his skill in detailed observation in the description of "a mere laborer":

His covering is a sheepskin cloak, the wool inwards, lapping over in front, and kept together by a coarse and often colored girdle. It is dirty beyond conception, smeared with grease and smells most offensively. He wears a hat of no shape, with the band drawn tight half-way in the crown. His feet are hid in a sort of matting, composed of strips about an inch wide and plaited in the form of a moccasin. His beard hangs a foot from his chin. His mustache is thick and conceals both lips, and his hair, coarse and matted, is cut close and round, just along the rim of the hat. His neck is entirely bare, and his skin is everywhere pallid, hard, and dusty. This is an exact delineation of the mass of serfs and peasants whom you meet by the thousands at work along the wharves, or in the public buildings, or at highways. They are literally "hewers of wood and drawers of water" (26–27).

Dallas probably kept a diary at several points during the time between his two major periods of diplomatic service, but little of this material survives. One brief diary covers a few months at the end of his term as vice-president (December 4, 1848–March 6, 1849). This record includes interesting entries on the California gold rush and a particularly complimentary entry on Zachary Taylor, who had just been elected president as the candidate of the rival Whig party.[24]

The Democratic party returned to power with the election of Franklin Pierce in 1852, and in 1856 Dallas succeeded Buchanan as ambassador to the Court of St. James. In his English diary Dallas was again captivated by the grandeur of royalty. His first entry (December 3, 1857) describes "the opening of Parliament by the Queen in . . . a handsome and suggestive ceremony." Dallas remarked that "its chief charm arose from its being headed by an exemplary lady not yet old enough to have lost her grace and beauty," but he spends more space on the pomp of the ceremony and the extravagance of the queen's attire, including the "crown of brilliants, and jewels [that] sparkled all over her person" (218). The first pages of this section of the diary include more comments on gossip and ceremonies than on diplomacy and politics. However, Dallas shows us that much of importance can be learned from such sources. For example, he first learned of the fall of a British government while he was attending a royal dinner. First, "the Duke of Wellington . . . whispered . . . that the cabinet had resigned," and this news was followed by other "careless" remarks among the guests. Dallas was surprised that in the court this "great change in the administration of the Empire" which might "convulse the nation, and lead to a general European war," was used only to point to some moral or to adorn a tale, and so was "acknowledged only by a few smiles and jests" (243–44).

Dallas's English diary contains accounts of a number of interesting events, such as the completion of a transatlantic telegraph linking Britain and America. However, much of the material in this portion of the diary is stiff, lacking not only a special style, but also a sense of personal concern or unifying direction. The subject that gradually gave the diary such concern and direction was the series of events that would eventually lead to the Franco-Prussian War and to World War I: "Hungary is on the eve of revolt, Denmark is arming to maintain her rights in Schleswig and Holstein, Italy, under the magnificent inspiration of Garabaldi . . . [takes actions that make] war upon Austria seem inevitable, and it cannot fail to draw into its vortex Russia, Prussia, Germany, and, not impossibly Turkey." In addition Dallas noted "the military avalanche which a breath from Louis Napoleon may precipitate cross the Rhine. . . . Where on the face of the earth can the stranger, Peace take up her permanent abode?" (430–31).

Dallas was principally concerned with the growing sectional conflict in America that would culminate in the Civil War. An early sign of this concern comes in the entry for December 17, 1858, in which he expresses his dismay at the publication in the London *Times* of a letter from President Buchanan. Dallas makes the growing tension between North and South more vivid by comparing the president's public admission of the growing antagonism to the public airing of a marital dispute: "As there are secrets between man and wife which cannot be conversed about without stimulating the gossip and slander of their neighbors, so there are defective points in the manners and practices of a portion of every people which however anxious to correct them should never undergo exposition in the face of [other] nations eager to condemn all indiscriminately" (303).

Almost a year later Dallas noted the first news about John Brown's raid at Harper's Ferry. In June, 1860, he recorded the nomination of Lincoln and six months later news of the reaction to Lincoln's election: "The political storm rages fiercely in the South, taking a reckless direction for secession, and produces a financial panic which cannot pass away without effecting widespread ruin." Dallas tried to take a position between the strong abolitionists, whom he called "Garrisonian Radicals who denounce the Constitution as a 'League with hell'," and the pro-slavery agitators, whom he labeled "uniformly violent, effervescing, and unsuccessful ranters." Failing to find any "staid, judicious statesmen" in the South, Dallas expressed his fear that the Union would be lost (420–21).

On May 1, 1861, he recorded the news that Charles Francis Adams was on his way to become the new ambassador. Dallas was not unhappy about the end of his travels and the diary that focused on them. He had only a few days before written of his increasing difficulty in maintaining a regular diary and of his willingness to leave a country which "while commanding my highest admiration, I find after five years of trial, I do not and cannot like" (442). In his last entry Dallas wrote that Lincoln had issued a "proclamation against the seceding states as insurrectionary . . . [following] the fall of Fort Sumter." In his last lines he lamented, "My poor country can henceforward know no security or peace until the passions of the two factions have covered her hills and valleys with blood and exhausted the strength of an entire generation of her sons. All Europe is watching with amazement this terrible tragedy" (443).

Benjamin Moran (1820–1886)

Most of the extant portion of Moran's diary covers the period from 1857 through 1874, during which the diarist served as assistant secretary and then secretary of legation at the American embassy in London. Moran served under six ambassadors: James Buchanan, George Mifflin Dallas, Charles Francis Adams, John Lothrop Motley, Reverdy Johnson, and General Robert C. Schenck. He had earlier served Buchanan as private secretary and clerk starting in 1854, and there are indications in the surviving portions of the diary that he kept a record of that period as well.[25] He also kept a diary before his diplomatic service. Little of that work remains, but some of it formed the basis for a travel book: *The Footpath and Highway or Wanderings of an American in Great Britain in 1851 & 1852*.[26] The most historically important portion of Moran's diary, that covering the years leading up to and including the Civil War, has been published; a significant portion, however, remains only in manuscript.[27]

Although Moran spent over half of his life abroad, most of that in England, his self-image was still that of an American. And although a few Englishmen knew as much about the landscape and customs of Britain as he did, he never really felt a part of British life but, rather, a spectator of it. Part of this attitude may have resulted from the fact that because of his diplomatic post he was invited to many exclusive political functions and royal entertainments, while his social rank and economic status kept him from personal involvement.

At court functions Moran would often "amuse" himself by looking "for distinguished men" and women, recording in his memory the long list of observations and reactions that he would later write into his record. One moment his subject might be Queen Victoria herself: "I took a good look at the Queen and can speak of her personal appearance from close observation. Her skin is coarse, but she is, for all that, pretty! . . . Her manner is wonderfully natural and sometimes she turns her eyes up with an expression of girlish simplicity." The next moment he might shift his attention to some old "judge from Australia," who in his confusion almost leaves the room before his turn to be knighted (1:76–77).

Though Moran could move easily among the members of this aristocratic society, he was temperamentally apart from them. Of one royal ball he wrote, "Dancing, gay dresses, music, royalty, gilding, and small talk are things one tires of, and I got away after a decent time to wander through the cool picture galleries where the wind fanned the flowers and shook out their sweet perfume & dashed it along the newly matted corridors over the few saunterers who like myself preferred art to show and sweet air to the unwholesome atmosphere of a thousand tainted breaths and two thousand bitter bodies" (1:341).

Moran could be especially critical of the nobility. While he admired some of those in high stations, he was always on the lookout for those whose natures were at odds with their positions, and he seems to have been proud when he could point out their flaws, as he did in declaring that one "much admired" countess betrayed "the strongest expression of an intense love of admiration and cold, heartless selfishness and self worship I ever saw on one of God's creatures" (1:94). In another entry he first told how "Court ladies twittered and smirked, as if to do so were good manners," and then commented that, while "kitchen girls would not be guilty of" such improper behavior, "ladies in waiting can do anything, but honest labor" (1:317).

To a great extent such comments stem from Moran's pride in America's democratic ideals. When the queen refused to grant an audience to Franklin Pierce, Moran complained in his diary, "Had he been a miserable German Prince, a special royal train would have been sent to him & the hospitalities of the Court would have been his. But being nothing but the Ex-President of the greatest Republic that ever existed, he has no honors paid him" (1:572).

It is important to note that Moran's concerns were more with class than with national distinction. Among his harsher portraits is that of a wealthy girl from New York who, though elegantly dressed, had "a muddy complexion, dirty hair, and excessive silliness of manner." Moran went on to tell his diary that while this woman was so bashful that she "had well nigh fainted before the ceremonies were ended . . . such people will be presented" (1:317). Elsewhere in the diary he condemned the "Philadelphia snobbism quite offensive to me" of a young American doctor.[28] This "proud, dogmatical fool," had snubbed his own wife's sister's husband because that man had "no family history" (1:101). The personal motives behind Moran's reaction is apparent later in this entry when he compared this snobbery to treatment he felt he had received from the Dallases, who, he claimed, "always pass me by from coldness, and deprive me of the just honors of my place" (1:101).

The social class origins of Moran's democratic sentiments are obvious in his comments to a visitor from Philadelphia who remarked on the improvement of that city. Moran first asked if the man was referring to the condition of the buildings or the people, and when the visitor indicated the former, Moran replied that this "improvement" was "not an improvement" but only a sign that American cities were "rapidly approaching those of Europe in classes of rich & poor. . . . On the one hand poverty, misery & crime are on the increase, riches and inhumanity on the other harden the heart" (1:14). In a later entry Moran condemned the "disgraceful fact" that "some young ladies in Philad^a have been guilty of running up bills for dresses alone that amounts to 3000 to 4000 dollars in six months!" He found the "pride, idleness, extravagance and consequent disrespect for honest labor, which all of them sneer at," particularly repugnant because these were "republican daughters!"—the descendants of those who struggled in support of the Revolution. Clearly, Moran saw the Revolution as establishing the value of the ordinary citizen, and he suggested that the appropriate punishment for women who had so violated their nation's values would be to "set the lazy drones to work with scrubbing brushes" (1:167).

Moran was usually more interested in the people he met than in the places he went to see. Visiting the offices of the London *Times*, Moran found the printer who had worked at the paper when it was "worked off on hand presses at a rate of a token an hour . . . a greater curiosity than Applegarth's lateral press which prints 6,000 of the monster hourly" (1:33).

Moran excelled in his depiction of English customs, not only those practiced at the highest levels of English society, but also those of the common people so often ignored in the histories of a society. He gave an interesting description of *chaffing*, "a pastime peculiarly English. The passers call after the riders and the riders return the assault. All hands make offensive remarks in a pretended good humor, and sometimes very insulting things are said. Every folly is assailed, every thing singular is ridiculed. Women and men alike indulge in the nonsense and some of the *bon mots* are excellent. *Chaffing* if well done is excellent—to all but the unlucky butt of the joke" (1:52).

While Moran could play the tourist even in London where he lived and worked, he often had a "longing for a country ramble, for an opportunity of getting away for a few hours from the drudgery of diplomacy [and] from the smokey air of London" (2:1156). As a result, large portions of diary are tourist accounts of travels throughout that country, similar in pattern to the travel writing in *The Footpath and Highway*. Moran is a good guide, providing a wealth of information about such diverse matters as the origins of place names, the histories of obscure heroes, and numerous references to literature, so that minor attractions seem like major ones.

Typical of Moran's travel sections is one in which he and a friend travel to Kent to spend the weekend. The entry, of about thirty-five hundred words, begins and ends with incidents in London: stories about a practical joker that were told over dinner the night before the trip and his work on the day of his return (including the issuance of a passport to General Tom Thumb and dealings with a man who intended to import camels into Texas). These items help to frame the travel account by contrasting busy London with the calm of the country. Shortly after leaving a station crowded with "men women and children," Moran and his companion are walking "along a splendid road, the wind battling with the branches," a scene which prompts Moran to "wonder why modern artists always paint tame landscapes" (1:381–87).

Moran's own word paintings often depict calm and ordinary scenes such as a "vale studded with farms, and well wooded lands, fields of golden yellow grain, rich and gay," but they are frequently enlivened with language and observations that make them distinct: The inn where he breakfasted on "a pure country meal" served by a "laughing chambermaid" was "hung round with sporting pictures," and that where he dined was "such an inn as Chaucer doubtless stayed at on his famous trip to Canterbury" and "almost old enough to have had for guests pilgrims to 'A Becket's tomb" (1:382–84). Moran was an acute observer, noticing for his record such details as the ingenious design of a churchyard latch or an unusual epitaph. Everything seemed a subject for speculation and imagination.

Moran's diary is full of interesting character descriptions. He claimed that all small English towns "abound in original and extraordinary characters," and he cited several in his diary. In one he described "a fussy little fellow . . . probably 5 feet 2, and rotundity not far from the same measure. He was clearly a being of prodigious importance in his own opinion, and . . . he was promenading on the terrace which overlooks the sea, his eyes sweeping seaward with the air of a man learned in nautical matters, being doubtless able to distinguish a collier from a revenue cutter" (1:405). Like Sherlock Holmes, Moran made his character assessments on little information but with such style and conviction that the reader may be inclined to accept them without questioning the logical process that led to them.

Moran's character studies include many sharp comments on those with whom he came in contact. Surprised by the mild attitude toward England of the American secretary of state, Lewis Cass, Moran wrote, "the lion now roars you as gently as a suckling dove" (1:24). Moran called the American painter Miner Kellogg "a man of talents doubtless—but a bore withal" (1:73). He condemned Charles Francis Adams for behaving as "bearish as ever" because of his "usual surly humor" (8/1/66, 3/19/66). Ridiculing George Mifflin Dallas for subscribing to "a rabid journal taken mainly by publicans and known for that as the 'Swilltub,'" Moran commented, "I never take it up except with disgust" (1:321).

Moran saw his diary as preserving a historical record for later generations. Part of his conscious intent in keeping it seems to have been to create a document that might be used, as his earlier diary had been, as the basis for a travel book. The inclusion of gossip would help the sales of such a work. However, though his diary contains many gossipy stories of and comments on the people he encountered in his duties, he considered the publication of such material improper and certainly never intended these items to be made public.

In general, Moran believed that his "private or personal afflictions" were not the appropriate "subject matter of a journal" such as his (1:14). Yet, as with most diarists, Moran was his own most important character. Much of his self-portrait develops as part of his treatment of other subjects, but on many occasions he wrote about his personal rather than his professional life. One subject of personal concern that found its way onto his pages was the sickness and death of his wife, Catherine Goulder Moran, whom he had met during his early travel in England and married in 1851.[29] She was then already in her forties, ten years older than he, but, as the diary indicates, he was devoted to her.

At the beginning of the published portion of the diary Mrs. Moran was already struggling with an incurable illness: "Her sufferings are terrible; and I sometimes think it would have been a greater mercy to have permitted the disease to take its course and saved her the torture than to have resorted to the awful remedy she now suffers under" (1:40). He used the diary to record his wife's wish to die in his arms and his own willingness "to die with her *for* her if I could" (1:164, 167).

Moran devoted a long section of his diary to the period of his wife's death, writing, "I have lost part of myself and can never forget the trial. If ever a wife was attentive, mine was; and if ever a soul went to heaven it was hers. . . . had I to marry again she would be my choice. . . . Had she lived, my home would have been an earthly paradise" (1:168–69). After her death he continued to write of visits to her grave and other reflections on her.

In the face of Moran's devotion to his wife, the reader may be perplexed by his comments on a young lady named Alice Bird, particularly in two entries written before his wife's death: "Last night I had the pleasantest hour with dear Alice. How my soul clings to that dear girl" (1:114), and "I passed a pleasant hour with dear Alice last night and had a thousand kisses. When shall our walks be resumed?" (1:116). While suggestive, these items offer insufficient evidence for any conclusion about this relationship.[30]

Moran did have an eye for attractive women. In one entry he wondered how a "beautiful, luscious young Duchess" ever married "a rusty old fellow of 66 with a figure like a flour barrel" (1:502). In another, describing a visit to the House of Lords with the Dallas family, Moran first confessed his relief that the "ill concealed pride" of one of Dallas's daughters led her to reject his offer to escort her to the Ladies' Gallery and so spared him from "having such a mass of ugliness and bones on my arm." Then he remarked on the beauty of two other women there "whose glowing shoulders, fair faces, and heaving breasts would have tempted an angel" (1:633).

Moran did not confess everything to his diary. In one entry he mentioned "a vow which must follow me for good or evil through life," but did not record what it was. In another he wrote, "Last night was an adventure to me; but the secret must not be recorded" (1:641). The implication of such passages is that he considered the possibility that someone else would see his diary.

A large portion of the diary is devoted to Moran's official duties, including his attendance at debates in Parliament on issues vital to American interests and his handling of letters "from all parts of the earth" (1:73). Many of his duties, such as the copying of dispatches, were routine and tedious. One duty, frequently mentioned, was dealing with the many people who came to the embassy. Moran wrote, "It is impossible for me to describe the continuous line of visitors to me daily. . . . I talk with them, supply such information as I am able, and then let them go. . . . Although many of them state remarkable things in conversation, I have neither the ability to remember it all nor time to record it if I could" (2:1086).

Yet Moran recorded far more of such material than this statement suggests. Some of these visits would provide "a little piece of romance" to interrupt "the monotony of the daily routine." He recorded the visit of two brothers who came bearing a letter of introduction to a British lord. The letter had been given to one brother, a schoolmaster from Connecticut, by one of his employees, a teacher of modest income. These brothers had assumed the teacher to be an impostor because they could not believe that "an aristocrat might have in him enough of the democrat to follow a plebeian calling for an honest living." In telling the tale, Moran revealed his delight in exposing this prejudice by helping to prove that the honest American teacher was actually the brother of the English lord (2:1037).

Moran frequently had to deal with rude people demanding service, such as one "vulgar, ill-mannered, ill-behaved clown" from Boston, who "threw his ugly fleshy carcass into a chair as he entered, and his first salute was 'Visé my passport.'" While Moran was able to be diplomatic, his diary shows that he was not always willing to take such behavior quietly. When this same man proceeded to ask for advice and then announced his intention to ignore it, Moran "cooled him" by replying, "Gentlemen, when they ask for information know how to acknowledge the favor granted. I shall decline to give you further advice" (1:437).

Despite such routine duties, Moran considered himself more than a mere secretary and felt that his experience made him able to advise the ambassadors he served: "When Mr. Adams and I first talked about Lord Russell's note on the claims, I told him that the clause proposing a commission to which should be referred all the claims that have arisen during the late Civil War was a trick. I believed it to refer to British claims against us." Moran went on to show that while Adams "could not think the British Gov't so mean as to make such a proposition," later events allowed Moran to boast, "My view of the case was right" (10/14–17/65). Indeed, early in his own diary of his service as minister to Britain Charles Francis Adams wrote of Moran, he "is of great use to me. Indeed I know not how I should get on without him."[31]

Given his pride in his own ability, an ability that seems supported by the comments of others, Moran was especially affronted by what he took to be the prideful disrespect shown toward him by the ambassadors, their families, and their friends. Some of his strongest sentiments were directed against the family of George Mifflin Dallas; when they finally left England, Moran ended a diary notebook with an assessment of them:

I part with the whole lot with joy. A more heartless, selfish, cold-blooded and unprincipled set, I never knew. The women are too soulless to deserve respect. During my wife's illness they never asked about her health—a piece of brutality. . . . Geo. M. Dallas is a creature of his family. He is a weak, vain, man, with a certain amount of lawyer like talents, but is not a statesman. . . . For years he fed on the idea of being The President, and all his acts were to that end. Selfishness is the sin of his soul & hypocrisy a strong element in his nature.[32] . . . He is a contradiction. . . . Professedly a Democrat he is at heart an Aristocrat. . . . His son Phil is the most ill-mannered unprincipled beast I ever knew. He is a liar a coward and a brute. He would injure anyone to satisfy his own lust. (1:812)

In contrast to this condemnation of Dallas, Moran's initial reaction to Adams was positive. He praised Adams's "surprising knowledge of British politics" and declared that Adams "bids fair to be a useful minister." However, Moran still insisted that his own skills were better than those of the ministers he served. Called upon to copy Adams's first dispatch, Moran called it "not an able paper . . . [but] better than any Dallas ever wrote" (2:815). However, in the beginning of 1863 Moran began to record statements reflecting a change in his attitude toward Adams: "Mr. Adams is an opinionated and yet a timid man. For a year now he made a good Minister; but he is too much in love with himself to be useful" (2:1128). Perhaps the reason for his changed assessment was not any change in Adams's diplomatic skill but in a real or fancied change in Adams's treatment of him. A few weeks later he complained, "Mr. Adams exhibits now the most perfect indifference to the suggestions of his secretaries and in fact even sneers at them. 'Pish' is his common reply to everything we say!" (2:1139). When Richmond fell Moran contrasted his own exultation with Adams's "icy" reaction (2:1410).

Part of Moran's conflict with Adams seems to have stemmed from a sense of favors extended to Moran's subordinate, Dennis Alward. In describing this conflict in his diary, Moran offered unintended insights into his own character. A few entries after Moran noted, "Mr. Adams has taken Alward out to ride, but did not ask me to go." However, when, a few weeks later, Adams asked Moran to accompany him to "see the pictures at the water color gallery," Moran concluded the entry with, "This civility of Mr. Adams is a piece of sunshine. I am glad to have it in my power to give him credit for any show of courtesy to me" (2:1414).

Moran's forgiveness was short-lived. About a month later he complained, "Probably no minister ever more deliberately insulted his Secretary than Mr. Adams insults me. Today he took Alward with him to Twickenham . . . in his carriage before my face, and never said a word to me; but left me here to do slavish labor in the Legation. This studied incivility is worthy of an Adams, and no other person claiming the character of gentleman could be guilty of it" (2:1435–36). One can think of many reasons why Adams might have acted in this manner without intending any "insult." Among these might be the necessity to leave someone competent at the embassy. That Moran does not appear to have considered such possibilities is suggestive.

Less than a year later Moran's jealousy of Alward led to blows: "I told him [Alward] he was disrespectful to me and that he should have consulted with me before [leaving Adams's name]. . . . he was insolent, said I could not tell the truth, was a puppy and had quarreled with everybody in the Legation. . . . he tried to throttle me, threw me down and almost foamed at the mouth . . . but I would not and did not retract. A more disgraceful occurrence never arose in a Legation, and it will undoubtedly lead to my resignation. Adams will defend the scamp, and my self-respect will compel me to leave" (3/25/66). Moran later noted in his diary that, in fact, Adams supported him rather than Alward, but Moran did so without giving any indication that he had altered his belief in Adams's prejudice.

The most important historical events covered in Moran's diary are those concerning the Civil War. Though originally appointed by a Democratic administration, Moran believed that Lincoln's election would "prove a benefit to the nation" (1:745). And when news came of the secessionist movement, Moran condemned "the fanaticism of the slaveholders" which threatened to destroy the Union (1:759). When a

Southerner coming to the embassy for a passport flaunted his disdain for the Union, Moran responded that the Union would "flog you back to your duty & allegiance" (1:803).

For most of the war period Moran's concern was to keep Britain from acting in support of the Confederacy. When news came of the defeat of the Union army at Bull Run, he was not only dismayed by the victory of "the slave drivers and treason mongers" and the "cowardice and incompetency of many Union officers," but also by the reaction of the British: "Their long & loud professions of emnity to slavery are being belied by ill concealed delight at its success over bleeding freedom. The nation secretly longs for the dissolution of the Union, and are content to see slavery become a might power so that aim is accomplished" (2:858). He attacked the hypocrisy of the British newspapers that once "could not too loudly condemn slavery," but that had been so corrupted by Southern money that they saw "no great crime in the infamous system" (2:904). When the British press condemned the "Trent Affair," Moran wrote: "That pink of modesty and refinement, *The Times,* is filled with such slatternly abuse of us and ours, that it is fair to conclude that all the Fishwifes [*sic*] of Billingsgate have been transferred to Printing House Square to fill the ears of the writers there with their choicest phraseology" (2:917).

Moran served as secretary of legation in the London embassy long after the end of the war and the departure of Charles Francis Adams. On December 11, 1874, he recorded an item from the morning newspaper: "From our American Correspondent. . . . The President has appointed Benjamin Moran, Secretary of Legation in London, to be the United States Minister in Portugal." About the same time that he read this article he received the first letters about the appointment. Three weeks later Moran wrote in his diary that he was especially "proud of honor" because, as far as he could learn, it was "the first and only time . . . that an American Secretary of Legation . . . [had] been appointed to the post of minister" and that as such it was "the recognition of . . . services" that had "so long seemed unappreciated." However, while he maintained that this appointment was a "great distinction," in a manner typical of him he complained that he "should have preferred the Hague, a post which . . . [he regarded] as very far above Lisbon" (12/30/74). His feeling are further exposed in the entry written the next day: "This ends a year of grace, 1874. It has not been a very happy year to me; but it leaves me minister at the court of ~~St. James's~~ Lisbon instead of Secretary of Legation at the Court of St. James's" (12/31/74).[33]

Moran served in Portugal until 1882, but almost none of that period is recorded in his diaries. On March 2, 1875, he began a new volume, titling it "Journal of A Mission to Portugal." But he managed only a few entries; the rest of the pages are blank.

Chapter Seven
Generalized Life Diaries

While the life diaries in the previous chapter tend to focus on periods of travel and on the sense of dislocation caused by it, most life diaries provide no such emphasis. Even when, as we shall see in the chapter on Transcendentalist journals, a group of diaries are related by some interest of their authors, subject matter is not the motive for diary production. Rather, in the true life diary the habit of diary keeping itself is the motive; and, therefore, extensive diary production continues even when a diarist's activities change. Among the best of the generalized life diaries written in America during the last half of the nineteenth century are those of Charles Francis Adams, Sidney George Fisher, and George Templeton Strong.

Charles Francis Adams (1807–1886)

The diary of Charles Francis Adams would be an extraordinary document if only because of its size. It spans six decades, and for most of that period the almost daily, well-written entries average over two hundred words. Moreover, Adams's place as the son and grandson of presidents and his own prominent social and political position gave him a unique opportunity to record the development of the nation as he recorded his own development as an individual. Unfortunately, a sizable number of entries record repetitious routine activities. In a smaller diary these entries might be accepted for their contribution to the overall portrait, but in such a long diary they make it difficult to follow the major themes. The overall quality of Adams's diary makes this effort worthwhile but an abridged version would better serve the average reader.

Adams made an early attempt to continue the family tradition of diary keeping when he was only ten and another when he was twelve; however, except for an index of entries in January and February, 1820, no diary material survives before that titled "Journal of a Vacation Spent in Washington . . . from December 22nd. 1823 to February

20th, 1824."[1] In beginning the vacation diary, Adams declared that his purposes were the improvement of his writing and the preservation of experience for later reading; but though he was concerned with his style and had the opportunity to record events that would "have a material influence upon this country" (12/undated/23), most of this section has little literary value.

Most of Adams's "Diary of Events" (May 1–October 31, 1824) is little better, recording the diarist's work at college, such as readings and lectures. But in a period of vacation in late summer, 1824, Adams showed his ability to move away from dry, routine entries and write an interesting record. For example, on his seventeenth birthday he considered the division of his life between "thought" and "study" on the one hand, and "laziness," "folly," and "dissipation" on the other (8/18/24). This division of his world is a sign of his attempt to find some pattern in the experiences he recorded. In another entry of the same period Adams made a penetrating analysis of his parents' characters: "My mother is the same woman she ever was, as pleasing, and as lively. My father is, as usual, unpenetrating. . . . I can study his countenance for ever and very seldom can find any sure guide by which to move. . . . He makes enemies by perpetually wearing the Iron mask" (9/6/24).

On November 1, 1824, the day of the election that would lead to his father's selection as president of the United States, Adams began a new diary manuscript book.[2] Unfortunately, this book was lost, and only an index in diary form remains. The events of this period not only include those relating to his father's election, but also the ball at which Adams met his future wife, Abigail Brooks. Moreover, while the absence of entries of personal and historical importance makes the loss of this diary material regrettable, readers of Adams's diary should also be concerned because this period was pivotal in its development.

In a new diary book started in November, 1826, Adams re-created entries of early summer, including those dealing with the death of his grandfather John Adams. In starting this new book Adams declared that his diary had already become a "stiff [record] of what happens every day" written out of habit in a style that he found displeasing and that, although the period had been a particularly happy and eventful one, "the passions and feelings of so young a man . . . [could] interest only himself" (11/26/26).

The next years of the diary include some interesting and important sections, such as that relating to Charles's marriage to Abigail Brooks.

The most significant deal with Adams's relationships with his brothers and his father because they reveal what would continue to be one of the most important themes in the diary, the conflict between Adams's desire to be thought able to assume the family commitment to national leadership and his dislike or even fear of the burden of such responsibility. In entries written in 1829 we see his reactions first to the unexpected death of his eldest brother, George, "either accidentally or in a fit of derangement . . . from the deck of the [steamship] Franklin" (5/2/29), and then to a note written by George asking Charles to convey money "to a little girl whom he [George] had seduced and who was then pregnant by him" (5/13/29). Charles may have shared his mother's belief that George's death was the result of family pressure to succeed, and almost certainly Charles was beginning to glimpse the internal and external forces leading him to assume responsibility (2:401n).

Charles's relationship with his brother John also advanced the theme of responsibility. Charles had complained that John had regularly, "unjustly and unnecessarily" treated him with a "galling sense of inferiority," treatment which seemed to suggest that he was less worthy of the Adams name (8/28/33). The brothers were reconciled, but on October 23, 1834, John died. Traveling to Washington after John's death, Adams wrote an entry that revealed one part of his feelings toward his obligation as an Adams, an obligation which, after the death of his brothers, had descended to him alone:

How cheerless and barren everything looked, how desolate now, where formerly the anticipation of youthful vacations and all the novelty of fashionable life had thrown a glow of cheerfulness. Both my brothers with whom I shared all these hopes and feelings gone, corrupted by the very luxury we longed for. . . . My situation in life now removed from all prospects of ambition, and from scenes of exalted intrigue. What is Washington to me now, but the monument of my father's disappointment, the grave of my brothers and the memorial of most of the misery and all of the vice of my own past life. (11/15/34)

While this entry suggests that Adams was willing to avoid the pursuit of ambition, other entries reveal an unwillingness to ignore what he saw as his responsibilities. For example, when his attempts to save his parents from "anxiety and distress of mind for the future" were rejected, and he was "called upon merely to render menial services," Charles used his diary to record his "bitterness" and "disappointment."[3]

Indeed, Adams felt that his obligations as a son offered him no other place to express his resentment. Though sorry to see his father "so bowed down," he made a point to declare in the diary, "I have contributed less to this than any member of the family. I have served him as well as I could although I had heretofore thought myself not cherished as I might have been." Adams was particularly distressed by his father's declaration that *"property* had ceased to interest him" and that even the family estates at Quincy including "his own residence and that of his father before him might as well go" (11/17/34). To Charles, these statements seemed not only to show a lack of "sensitive feelings" toward himself and his children, but also to threaten his right to be proud of his heritage as an Adams.

Unfortunately for the literary quality of the diary, items such as these constitute only a tiny fraction of Adams's record of this period. His typical diary entry for most of the two decades following the resumption of the diary in 1826 was of even more modest quality. Though of reasonable length, it was briefer than that of the early diary and, more significantly, it was fixed in a rigid pattern. Most entries begin with statements about the weather and a trip to the office, include comments on Adams's reading, writing, routine business, and relaxation, and conclude by indicating that the evening had been spent at home. If Adams took a walk, he would write only "took a walk," as if the sights, thoughts, and feelings he experienced during the walk were too ordinary to merit recording.

Adams might write, "My Diary is my companion. I unburden my sorrows and communicate my joys, I express my hopes and display my fears" (1/1/33), but the pages of this portion of his diary show little such material. More frequently, he admitted that his life had become mired in the routine and the ordinary and that, as a result, the diary had lost much of its intrinsic merit. In one entry he wrote: "My Diary is a pretty monotonous record of the very tenor of my life. I believe it is of use to a man to accustom himself to keep one, but the profit is not attached to the record itself so much as the ease it gives to one's pen" (2/6/32). Two and a half years later he complained, "I am ashamed of my Diary and myself. Never was my diary so perfectly uninteresting and never was I so much tempted to close its pages forever" (10/17/34). These feelings about the diary were not confined to a brief period of discouragement, but rather were repeated in entries written over a wide period. At one time he wrote, "My personal situation changes little, so little that a record ceases to possess any interest and yet I grow older" (9/1/37), and at another, "My daily life has so much monotony in it that I hardly feel it worthwhile to continue my record" (11/28/37).

It is important to note that in each of these entries Adams was not really complaining against his diary, but rather, as in the following excerpt, condemning his mundane existence: "Sat down with my perseverance to writing—But what should I write without a subject? What good is to be expected from any effort of mine. My time is better employed digging the earth as I do in the afternoon" (9/4/37). The death of his brothers, George in 1829 and John in 1834, had left him the responsibility of carrying on the Adams tradition, "the only representative in my generation of the distinguished branch of the name," but instead of acting he found himself "wound up in the interest of merely domestic affairs . . . [and] vegetating in a useless hot-bed of enervating luxury" (11/1/34). What had an Adams or the diary of an Adams to do with an afternoon devoted to carting gravel or a morning spent fishing? (10/9/37, 10/2/37).

The years passed and with them his hope of fulfilling his role as an Adams, but Charles recognized that his efforts had not been without result; he had won for himself "the good opinion of those whose good opinion is worth mentioning" (1/1/38). This "good opinion" was an asset that could be used as Adams became increasingly interested in politics. The diary shows signs of his changing interests, especially his involvement in the growing controversy over slavery. He had long been concerned about the effect of slavery in the South, but now even his native Boston seemed "corrupted heart and soul by the principles of slavery" (12/8/37).

In the last half of the 1830s Adams became more willing to enter into public affairs, the while he still refused to accept a formal political role, by 1836 he had become "so interested in observing the course of the political affairs of the Country that it . . . [took him] an hour of every morning to look over the newspapers" (2/10/36). In 1837 he gave his first public lecture and, when his efforts gained little notice, he questioned, "Are people afraid to praise me, or do I not deserve it? Is there a determination to blast my honest attempts at reputation by honest silence or is it a trial of my temper for the purification of my overweening self conceit?" (11/20/37). This interest in a political role seems to have coincided with the improvement of the diary as a work of intrinsic value, not only because it discussed more interesting events, but also because, as the diarist came to consider his life important, he placed more value on its record. Reviewing his life at the beginning of a new diary volume, Adams took the "opportunity to moralize upon the passage of the years," and concluded that he had done little for himself or mankind: "I have picked a little hole in the sand wherein I have attempted to lay a small store for future use, altogether doubtful whether they will prove more than a buried treasure. . . . Favored as I have been more than is common, I have gathered only here and there a light fagot, where I might have got a tree" (1/1/39). However, until 1840 he rebuffed repeated attempts by the Whig party to nominate him as their candidate for the state legislature (10/30/39). The process of internal consideration and external pressures leading to Adams's eventual decision to accept the nomination forms one of the more interesting "chapters" of the diary.[4]

The succeeding years of the record show Charles's increasing involvement in politics; and when he left the legislature in 1845 he had already established his position as "one of the recognized antislavery leaders in the state."[5] However, he continually expressed his wish to leave public office, and finally refused to run in 1845. It was not until the death of his father left Charles Francis Adams as *the* representative of his family that he completed his transformation into a national political figure and his diary's transformation into an effective autobiographical document.

Reacting to the claim by members of the Whig party that there was no longer any living Adams to trouble them, Charles wrote in the diary of his determination "to trouble the profligate politicians as his father had done before him" and declared: "It has been the fate of three generations of our race to stand as the guardians of Liberty in this Commonwealth against the corrupting principles of a moneyed combination. My trial is now, and they may be able to crush me by their insolence, but it shall not be without a struggle. So long as I live there shall be an Adams in this Commonwealth who will denounce every bargain to trade away the honor of his country" (9/14/48). From this point on, Adams seemed to find everything pointing to some higher destiny and directing him to action. Even the sermon he heard the next Sunday, "He hath remembered his covenant," seemed "remarkable in its application to myself in this present struggle" (9/17/48).

While Charles tried to assume his father's political role, he made no sudden change in either his life or his diary to imitate his father's example. Entries still began with references to the weather and continued with rather ordinary events, such as time spent listening to his children reading from the Bible on Sundays. At one point Adams claimed that he had become so indifferent to diary keeping that even though that week's events seemed "unusually worthy of notice," he delayed buying a new manuscript book after filling his current one (9/1/50).

Political concerns became more prominent in his entries, and the theme of such passages was that Adams was being called to action. Writing that there was a "development of public opinion in favor of our cause," he concluded, "It needs only the requisite amount of intellectual force to produce the greatest political revolution since 1776" (9/30/48). One implication of this conclusion was that Charles might have the opportunity to repeat the successes of his grandfather John Adams.

Even his work in reading and editing family papers, including the diaries of his father and grandfather (an effort that would consume much of his time for over thirty years), served to reinforce Adams's understanding and conviction of his place in a family destiny. Reading John Adams's diary, Charles remarked that its words might "well weigh upon his descendants" (12/21/48). These diaries also served to give Charles a better sense of history and of the value of the diary form for those who help to shape history. However, his own actual involvement in politics was still limited. While he gradually became more involved in Free Soil politics, he often used the diary to complain about political "treachery" and to express a wish "to cut loose as much as possible from party associations" (2/12/51). Nevertheless, each personal attack ultimately reinforced his determination to fulfill the family obligation for service.

Adams typically closed and opened the diary for each year with reflections on the past and expectations for the future. On New Year's day, 1856, he wrote: "I open with this day a new volume of what has become an extended though monotonous record. If it contains no great share of adventurous activity of life it is happily free from all traces of its great vice or crimes. I trust I am grateful for this blessing of my lot that I have not been led into temptations too great for my strength— May the blessing of the future prove not less favorable to me than the past." While Adams looked back on a period of relative inactivity, he did not realize that the coming year would mark the beginning of a significant increase in his political involvement or that with such involvement his diary would take on increased importance, not just as a record of the most important part of his career, but also as a place in which to consider his course of action.

The diary for 1856 shows that while Adams still avoided involvement he was becoming more ready to act. An entry written shortly before the election of 1856 gives another powerful example of the way he used his diary to express an overt wish to be free from politics while betraying an inner desire to be a successful politician. Anticipating a defeat for the Republicans and a victory for "the slave power," Adams wrote:

I mourn for my country which seems to be rapidly changing the essence, if not the form of government, and forgetting the first purpose of its creation. But to me this event makes little difference. A close observation of the current affairs has convinced me that the day has gone by for the success in political life of men formed on the general basis on which I have chosen to rest myself. It has been therefore rather the act of a kind providence to put in my way at this time obstacles to an entrance into public life. (10/17/56)

When the actual vote took place, Adams wrote of his happy surprise to learn his party "had swept the state from end to end by a prodigious vote as well as all of New England" (11/5/56). He saw this change in his political fortunes as a sign that his family was regaining public respect and a potential for a return to political prominence (2/20/57). On October 7, 1858, Adams recorded the "marvelous result to me" that he had been nominated for election to Congress. On election day he wrote, "My mind never was more easy, a fact [for] which I can scarcely account to myself. Perhaps the reason is my feelings have been much soothed by the general manifestation of kindness and esteem which has been elicited in the entire canvas that I regard success in the election as more or less certain" (11/2/58). Though the next day he "awoke . . . with a sense of some anxiety," fearing that he was "not made by nature for the turmoil of contentious activity," he felt easier after the newspapers showed that he had won by a comfortable margin (11/3/58).

Adams had no personal desire to go to Washington, and if anything the fact that he and other members of his family had once lived there served to make the prospect more unattractive. After passing the house in which his family had lived, Adams wrote in his diary that his principal impression was "rather like that from a disturbed dream than of any agreeable kind because the memories reinforced the sharp contrast between the life he had chosen and the political life his father and grandfather had led: "My own life has been so different, and for the most part so tranquil and happy that I shudder at the returning to this opposite mode of existence. It is all so hollow, so tempestuous, so full of evil passions, so disappointing to the most laudable ambition. Let me console myself with the hope. however faint, that I may do some good. . . . Political struggles have become so distasteful to me that I may retire from them" (9/9/59). Adams seems to have been convinced that he would face the same problems and suffer the same pain that his father had. Indeed, shortly afterward he reread the part of his father's diary that covered his years as secretary of state and president, confident that this record held "the clue to all our later political movements" (9/30/59). The action shows Adams's sense of the importance of the diary form.

The most significant event of that year was John Brown's raid, for it produced a widespread awareness of an impending conflict between North and South. Although Adams was only a freshman Congressman, he sensed that he was destined to play a major role in that conflict and worried about his ability: "My mind is somewhat weighed down by the prospect of my situation. I see very clearly the path which I ought to follow, but it requires a degree of self command of which I am not sure. The onslaught of Brown and the panic it has excited in Virginia will affect the elections of the year in order to uphold for one more term the dominion of the Oligarchy. The true mode of defeating all the plots and of placing the cause of freedom in an advantageous light before the people and the world is the object to be sought. Am I equal to this great task?" (11/24/59)

The diary of this period is full of interesting accounts of fierce sectional rivalry on the floor of Congress. One Southern congressman made a "general and vulgar denunciation of all the Republicans, as knaves, and traitors and deserving of the gibbet. He threatened that . . . the power of government should be used to crush them" (12/8/59). Another, in a more "gentlemanly manner . . . declared his conviction that the election of any Republican like Seward or Chase to the Presidency according to the Constitutional forms would be a justifiable cause for the dissolution of the Union"(12/10/59). Adams himself was able to use language effectively against his political opponents: in one passage he called a fellow congressman "one of the slimy brood of demagogues of the Free States still striving to hold his chin above water by the aid of a government in its present pro-slavery hands" (12/15/59).

Adams's account of the political infighting and manipulation both in Congress and behind the scenes is excellent and extensive. Certainly his depiction of the workings of Congress is far longer and better written than that in the diaries of his father and grandfather. One series of entries extending for almost two months details the voting and manipulation about the election of a new Speaker of the House.

In the spring of 1860 Adams wrote of the split in the Democratic party and the nomination of Lincoln by the Republicans. He recorded that he was depressed by the nomination because he thought that the party owed it to Seward and because he feared that it was a sign "of the timidity of the middle states who want to avoid forcing the slavery question." He considered Lincoln "a fair representative . . . honest and tolerably capable, but . . . [with] no experience and no business habits" (5/18/60). However, for Adams the system itself was more important than the man who was elected. On the day of Lincoln's election Adams not only remarked on his belief that the election would be "the first step toward the reform of a shockingly corrupt system of the Slaveholding Oligarchy," but also on the "remarkable idea . . . that all over this broad land at this moment the process of changing the rulers is peacefully going on" (11/6/60). He reacted to secession in terms of its basic distrust of that democratic, constitutional process (11/11/60).

Adams was fearful that Lincoln was not equal to the challenge before him, lacking "the heroic qualities which he most needs" (2/21/61). However, Adams doubted his own ability to endure such a challenge. Hearing the speculation that he might be appointed secretary of the treasury, he not only denied any "desire for the post," but also insisted that, despite "the honor of such an appointment," he did not wish to undertake "the heavy responsibilities that weigh upon the president's advisors" (1/3/61, 11/23/60). Adams gives an excellent portrait of the beginning of Lincoln's administration, including a description of the inauguration, "grand in its simplicity," that offers an interesting depiction of the characters: Buchanan looking "old and worn out," Lincoln "awkward and out of place" (3/4/61). However, more important in the course of the diary are incidents that of themselves have little historical importance but that help to give a feeling for the historical period. For instance, he tells how, after seeing some troops "marching to and fro," he went to "the least frequented parts of Georgetown and there in the quiet presence of nature tried to forget the turmoil of public affairs" (2/22/61).

When Adams learned that he "had been nominated as Minister to Great Britain," he explained that he did not know if he should "feel elated or depressed by this distinction" which would require great sacrifice for himself and his family: "In one sense it flatters my pride in that I make the third in lineal descent in my family, on whom that honor has been conferred by his country, an unprecedented case in American annals. On the other hand it imposes new and untried duties, and responsibilities of a grave character at this crisis which I may fail to meet" (3/19/61).

Arriving in England on May 5, 1861, Adams immediately faced a host of difficulties. His first objective, keeping Britain from recognizing the belligerency of the Confederacy, was lost even before he arrived at his post, and his other duties were complicated by Secretary of State Seward's "awkward brusquerie" that had offended the British prime minister (6/1/61). Moreover, Adams found himself without the network of acquaintances or knowledge of the "actual state of Europe" so necessary to his work (6/7/61, 7/6/61). When news came of the "disastrous defeat at Bull Run," Adams not only had to worry about his poor country," but also about "the satisfaction felt by many powerful Britains at America's 'humiliation'" (8/4/61, 8/6/61). He hoped that this attitude was not widespread and that he could appeal to "a leaven of better feeling in the great body of the [British] nation" (1/15/62).

The diary contains numerous examples of Adams's skillful diplomacy, perhaps the most interesting and most significant of which appears in a series of entries describing his response to a letter from the British prime minister "Lord Palmerston denouncing in no measured terms General Butler's proclamation[6] and the government of the United States for employing him." While the letter "was marked private on the outside and confidential within," it was so "offensive and insolent both in tone and manner toward the government," that Adams felt he had been made "the recipient of an insult to . . . [his] country." He recognized that the obvious courses of action were dangerous: "On the one hand it will not do for me to pass over such an act without some notice. On the other I must if possible avoid any step that leads to national difficulty at this crisis. The path is full of danger, and I must tread it calmly" (6/12/62). Adams responded to Palmerston, but only by asking clarification as to whether the note was public or private. He addressed his embarrassment about the substance of the letter to Lord Russell, the foreign minister, explaining, "I could not for a moment imagine that Lord Palmerston would seek any concealment from him" (6/13/62). In this way Adams attempted to pit the two ministers against each other and put them on the defensive. The final result was that Russell declared that "the thing was altogether irregular, and could be regarded only as a private proceeding" (6/19/62). Russell's declaration not only gave Adams "great relief" but allowed him to recognize that he had "all the advantage" by turning aside the possibility that Butler's proclamation could be used as an excuse for the British to support the Confederacy (7/4/62).

Adams struggled against growing opposition until the fall of 1862, when he recorded the "exciting" news that Lincoln had issued the Emancipation Proclamation. Adams saw this event as part of a divinely ordained plan, and expressed his conviction that the war might have been "a just judgment upon the country for having puttered with the evil [of slavery] for so long" (10/22/62). Adams still had misgivings about the war effort—indeed, he had "dismissed all expectations of success"—but he now could write of his hope that "the principle of emancipation has got such hold that it can not again be eradicated. With this secure we may possibly be safe in future against repetition of this evil. Without it we shall continue to tread on coals" (1/29/63).

Certainly the Emancipation Proclamation made Adams's tasks in England much easier. He began to write that "great things are happening here" as the newspapers and public meetings provided a clear indication that, moved by this endorsement of emancipation, the "spirit of the middle classes" in England had turned to support the Union (1/30/63). On the second anniversary of his departure for England, he could write: "The interval has been on the whole the most difficult part of my life. I can only congratulate myself that I have safely got thus far, and look forward to the time now very rapidly approximating when my term of office closes" (5/1/63).

Adams still had problems; a good portion of his energy was spent on seeking to gain "reparations for the damages done by the ravages of the Alabama" and to prevent the building or release of other such ships (11/19/62). Moreover, as his work in England grew easier, he increasingly turned his attention to the war in America. He wrote of reports he received about political intrigues and attributed the lack of progress in the war to "the erring judgment from an incompetent but well meaning head . . . and the absence of a good military leader" (12/31/62). Typically, his concerns about the competence of the president and his generals ended with a statement such as the following: "On the whole I trust that the Divine Being will guard us better than we do ourselves and evolve out of this confusion some blessed result" (2/16/63).

Adams's routine duties, such as meetings with official visitors, the preparation of dispatches, and the delivery of speeches, fill many pages. These sections are not as interesting as they might have been because he disliked many of these duties and made no attempt to hide his distaste for them. He found "the most trying of a minister's duties" was "the social part" because his own "natural inclinations . . . [were] so very strong towards retirement." He found public ceremonial speeches "painful," especially when faced with "carping critics" (2/21/62).

Of course not all of Adams's time was spent on official duties. He recorded news of his family or work on his coin collection, and visits to museums, art galleries, plays, and concerts (4/14/62). He also spent a good deal of time visiting churches. In one excursion Adams, inspired by his readings from "Pepys's quaint and amusing Diary," went to visit "St. Olave's church in Hart Street, which escaped the great fire." Unfortunately, he found that "its antiquity . . . [had] been interfered with by repairs," leaving little that reminded him of Pepys's description (5/29/64).

Adams was interested in those "little things that give to the City its distinguishing interest" (5/29/64). He liked to explore those parts of London not usually frequented by tourists, and wrote of "rambles through the alleys and byways of the city" after days at work. He saw "a remarkable contrast to the fashionable portion. . . . Few vehicles, poor shops, dirty children playing about the lanes and alleys, and here and there ragged men and women, but extreme quiet withal, and nothing indicating crime or vice. . . . the extremes of society are here in terrible proximity" (6/11/61).

Adams also made numerous trips away from London, visiting such sights as Cambridge, "chief nursery of [Massachusetts's] original preachers" (8/12/61), and Edinburgh, associated in his mind with the poetry of Sir Walter Scott (8/8/63). He saw the hot springs at Bath, Welsh castles, and picturesque English country seats. He also made trips to the Continent.

Adams had purchased an unusually large manuscript book for his diary in England in the hope that it would serve him for his entire term as ambassador, but in May, 1864, he found it necessary to begin another with little hope that he might be able to return home before it was full (5/1/64). However, only a month later Adams had heard of Union victories that suggested the war might be coming to an end (6/4/64). By the end of 1864 he recognized that the peril of the Union was over. Soon he was able to record a number of favorable events "details which show Sherman's march to have been one of the most brilliant and successful movements in history" (1/1/65), signs of favor from the British government, "extracts from the Southern press" that seem like "a convulsive groan which would excite pity if not mixed too much with desperation of passion" (3/13/65), and, finally, news of the fall of Richmond—which led Adams to be confident of "a termination of the struggle so long foreseen and dreaded about the slave element in our system" (4/15/65).

While the success of the Union seemed certain, the fate of individual soldiers was still in doubt, and Adams began to worry over the fate of his son Charles, who was an officer in the Union Army. Only after he finally received news of Lee's surrender did he allow himself to feel "at ease," confident that all was well in America (4/23/65). However, even this confidence seemed premature as Adams received word of the assassination of the president. Adams recorded his shocked reaction to the news, but the primary emphasis of the entry is on the meaning of the act in a broader historical context. He wrote, "I could not but see that this was only a legitimate sequence to the origin of this rebellion. It is fitting that what began with perjury, fraud and treachery should end in private assassination. Such is the fruit of the seed that was sown in slavery of the African race." While Adams had long questioned Lincoln's ability, he now declared, "There was a grandeur about the national government under his direction which he might not have been fully able to sustain, but which his successor will not attempt to continue. For his own fame the President could not have selected a more happy close. The just doubts about his capacity for reconstruction are scattered to the winds in the solemnity of the termination. From that moment his fame becomes like that of Washington the priceless treasure of the Nation" (4/26/65).

Adams's concerns at the time of Lincoln's death were already turning back toward America. While he believed that his English diary was probably "the record of the most important and interesting" period of his life, he increasingly felt that his life itself was "wearing away . . . with little satisfaction to myself or profit to the public" (7/31/66). With the war over, Adams used his diary to complain about having to remain in England and to express his longing for America. He had long wished to resign his post, and with the war over he felt that his continuation in his post was no longer essential. He regretted the loss of opportunities at home in America: "I am now conscious of an almost steady depression of spirits such as I never before had in my life. The cause, I think, is the utter want of interest I feel in everything around me and the sense that my absence from home is working unfavorably to most of my children and my property. Political views have no connection with it, for I look for relief only in the absence of them. Indeed, to me there is nothing to be gained by any change" (7/24/65).

Tired of the legation, which had become a "Castle of Indolence," Adams took longer and more frequent periods of vacation (1/4/67). His diary includes accounts of extended residences in the countryside and tourist trips in England and Ireland. He even wrote Secretary Seward "requesting a leave of absence for a short excursion to the Continent" (6/21/66). Toward the end of September, 1866, Adams left England for a trip to Europe. Unfortunately, much of the diary is taken up with relatively uninteresting accounts of paintings and churches.

The most important activity in this portion of the diary is the beginning of negotiations with Britain on America's claim for damages done to its commerce by the Confederate raider *Alabama*. On a personal level, Adams considered these negotiations important because they kept him from resigning his position. When a stalemate occurred in the negotiations, he wrote that it removed "the last real obstacle to my getting away from here, on the ground of any usefulness I may be of. Were everything quiet and established at home I would resign at once" (6/5/67).

Finally he was able to resign and begin preparations for his departure home to America. Adams, who had struggled for acceptance during his first years as minister, now wrote of a "handsome allusion made to me [in Parliament that was] . . . received with general cheers from all sides of the House" (3/7/68) and a banquet in his honor: "As this scene was passing before my eyes, the reflection would press itself upon my mind, What am I that so many of the distinguished statesmen of this, one of the most noted countries in the world should do me such homage! . . . My duties had been mainly to complain and find fault, and my satisfaction now consisted in the fact that I had faithfully complied with my instructions from home. . . . I want no better termination of my career" (4/1/68).

Adams's final official duty, a farewell audience with the queen, was marked by an uncharacteristic nervousness. It is the record of such personal reactions that make such scenes more than a record of dry formalities. Adams described himself as "much more agitated than . . . [he] expected" and noted that he almost made a severe diplomatic blunder by forgetting the correct form of address: "I . . . came very near saying your Highness and even your Worship which would have been very bad indeed." Fortunately, he survived the trial and could write in his diary, "I was once more a freeman" (5/13/68).

Freed from official responsibilities, Adams took the opportunity to do things he had neglected during his long residence, including a long-contemplated trip to see "the flowering of the horsechesnut trees" and a visit to Italy (5/3/68). He noted that he left for the Continent "just about the same hour that . . . [he had] arrived exactly the same day of the year seven years before" (5/13/68).

Adams embarked for his return voyage to the United States believing that "The seven years knot was completely cut," and that for the rest of his life Great Britain would only be "as a dream" (6/28/68). The next part of the diary is filled with those events and symbols that he believed would shape his life. Even the elements appeared auspicious, the calm sea and favorable winds advancing the progress of the ship (6/29/68). Certainly, Adams never again expected to fill his diary with accounts of political or diplomatic activity. Disembarking in New York while the Democratic nominating convention was meeting there, Adams showed no interest in becoming involved in American politics, and when he later received news of Grant's election, his reaction was to congratulate himself for "having been left out of the battle and conflict" (9/2/68). Examining his feelings two months after his return, he concluded: "The interval has changed me and all the circumstances around me to such an extent that the motions which formerly guided me and all the circumstances around me have in a measure lost their force. The question is only one of a few years during which my main duty must be to set my house in order rather than to contemplate enterprises. . . . My retirement from all connection with political affairs is absolute" (9/10/68).

Adams recorded no statement of enthusiasm at being back in America. His concern was for a quiet retirement. His principal reaction to finally returning to his home at Quincy was that, while "the old home looked much as it did," the intervening years since he left made him "feel much older than before." The change, Adams believed, was "rather in the state of mind than the body." He was still physically healthy, but his mind was in the conclusion of old projects rather than the initiation of new ones, "My active career has run its course and I must now prepare the winding up" (7/9/68).

Adams spent his time and diary on "the customary routine" (2/20/69). He wrote of cleaning his thermometer, restoring his cabinet, and working on his coin collection. He took walks, wrote letters, visited friends, saw to his accounts, and prepared his will (3/11/69). Even his old interest in reading and editing the papers of his family grew "more and more mechanical and uninteresting" (7/15/70).

One event that stands out in this section of the diary is the death of Adams's daughter Louisa. This series of entries is especially important because little of the diary is concerned with Adams's relationship to his family, and much of that is presented impersonally. However, the news of his daughter's death overwhelmed him. Adams described how in his distress he "rambled about for about an hour or more in the pasture now and then sitting down on a stone," trying in vain to gather his thoughts. Questioning his own motive in using the diary to relive "the hour of this agony," he tried to console himself with the thought that this affliction might be an attempt by the same God who had granted years of favors but now sought to remind him "of the fleeting nature of worldly prosperity and of the duty of preparation for another state." However, as Adams recalled his daughter's life, this concentration on spiritual lessons brought still more unease, leading him to make attempts to find excuses for conduct he had earlier found faulty. In a long moving portrait he tried to recall evidence that would excuse her failings:

Impulsive, wayward, passionate, yet generous affectionate and even heroic in her spirit, she often did foolish and indiscreet things which ran counter to the established notions of society. But her heart was always pure and her disposition heavenly. Her first disappointment was in her marriage, her second in the misfortune of the life of her first child, which prevented her from having more. Her husband though devoted to her and in the worldly sense all that could be desired wanted the capacity to lead her up to the level she was fitted by nature to occupy. . . . As a consequence she fell back to a life of frivolity and self indulgence to escape from ennui. . . . I think she had at her onset the opportunity to become the most accomplished as well as brilliant woman of her generation. (7/13/70)

Adams felt turned to stone, unable even to cry, perhaps because he worried about the "shortcomings and mistakes" he had made in raising his children (7/13/70, 7/14/70). The diary preserves his repeated attempts to both accuse and excuse himself for his daughter's frivolous behavior, including his concern that he had failed to adequately impress her "with the sentiment of religion." His only consolation was the hope that when faced with "the last agony" his daughter might have recalled early religious education and so have prepared her soul (7/14/70).

On August 8, 1871, Adams received "an official dispatch . . . announcing the wish of the President that I should act as arbitrator in the part of the United States at Geneva under the Treaty." Adams stressed that, while he considered the appointment to be an honor, he was accepting the task as a reluctant duty. Nevertheless he also betrays some pride in this recognition of past service:

It is not a duty in other respects desirable to me. It implies an interruption of my labors at home, and a couple of voyages with a winter spent in a city in no way remarkable for its attractions and a delicate responsibility withal. . . . Yet in spite of all this I am confronted with this public call for my services as I am thought better able to render them than most others, and what solid reason have I to meet it with a point blank refusal to serve? Is it laziness or cowardice or more inertia which is to justify such a step? I can recognize the propriety of neither pretense in my vocabulary . . . No, there is no path for me but the straight line of duty. (8/8/71)

On November 11, 1871, Adams parted from his wife and embarked for Europe, arriving in Geneva in the middle of December. When the talks were delayed Adams began a trip to Italy, but returned to the United States upon receiving the news that his wife had become ill at the prospect of his extended absence. As Adams was getting ready to return to Geneva, he received news that members of the splinter Liberal Republican party wanted to consider him at their convention in Cincinnati for the presidential nomination. Adams noted in the diary that he responded, "I could give no authority to any one to trade for me, and that I could not accept a nomination, if it was not unequivocally the sense of the assembly" (4/18/72). On arriving in Europe, Adams learned that he had narrowly missed being nominated. While his first reaction was "one of great relief in being out of the melee," his comment that "the governing party will of course exult a good deal, and it is I suspect a great escape for them" suggests that he still was caught between his wish for a calm private existence and his sense of his own potential for service (5/4/72).

Adams's portrait of the Geneva deliberations is full and interesting, ranging from a description of a dinner with the Prince of Wales to a record of the diplomatic manipulations that, thanks to Adams's efforts, ultimately produced a settlement (5/22/72). Some of the major pieces of evidence in the negotiations were Adams's own dispatches, and as he confided to his diary, he often had to proceed "without explicit instructions." Yet, when praised for his efforts, Adams would, after meditating, attribute his success "to a protecting care" that had done more for him than he sought or deserved (6/10/72, 7/4/72). This pattern is evident in several entries of this period. When one of the other arbitrators complimented him for "having saved the Treaty," Adams, after disclaiming special merit, "walked home musing on the strange results that attend human life" and expressed his surprise that, after having achieved all that he might expect and "when the termination of . . . [his] my career might be a blessing," he had the opportunity to be "an agent in terminating favorably a grave difference between great nations which has placed both of them under some sense of obligation to my poor labors" (8/29/72). After the closing ceremony, Adams walked home "musing . . . upon the remarkable dispositions of divine will which so often direct such remarkable effects through such feeble instruments." Attributing his success "to the disposer of events," he looked forward to the "honorable termination" of his "public career" (9/14/72).

Adams "bid Goodbye to Europe without a single regret . . . with no painful associations." After long wishing to leave it, he determined to consider it as "connected with the only brilliant part of my career" (11/3/72). Returning to America, Adams hoped to "have a right to rest" (11/13/72), but he soon heard speculation that he would be appointed secretary of state. Adams looked back at his earlier "escape . . . from a violently contested election for the Presidency" and was pleased when the appointment did not come (12/31/72). Afterwards he shrank from both "public life" and private "enterprises" (12/5/72).

The balance of the diary is a document of old age. Even though Adams lived many more years and retained a degree of political prominence few men achieve, his focus was away from involvement. Examining his diary, he noted that since his days passed "quietly in a pretty uniform course of occupation" there was "little to record" (2/1/73). He still followed politics, but he spent most of his time reading, writing, editing, and although he allowed himself to be nominated for several important offices, these nominations usually came without any effort on his part and without the likelihood of his election. Nominated for governor in 1876, Adams did not even vote for himself, writing in the diary of his "thanks to Divine Providence" for sparing him from the "dreaded" possibility of election (11/8/76). Afterwards, he remarked that he was content, for while public reaction showed his low "political standing," it revealed a high estimate of his "personal character." This personal esteem, he claimed, was all he had ever wanted. "For place in itself I never cared" (4/16/74).

Becoming aware that he was aging and that his "season of usefulness" was ending, Adams sought to avoid new projects and focus on "the execution of what remains uncompleted" (12/31/73). As in the following entry, Adams's vision was increasingly turned nostalgically toward the past: "The day was warm but the evening one of those exquisite scenes which we have at this time of year in perfection. I sat on the portico enjoying it all alone—And then I looked back on times long gone by when I had seen it with so many in the days of my grandfather, and again in those of my father. And lo here am I alone in their places!" (8/8/73).

One of his few public activities was his delivery of the official eulogy for William Seward, just one of the many acquaintances who died during Adams's final years. After attending services one Sunday, Adams remarked that "of the pews on the side that I sit as a head of a family there is not a single person left who was there when I was married . . . all disappeared, and others whom I do not know have come in to fill their places" (5/12/78). Adams had often devoted much of each Sunday's entry to a record of sermons and religious readings, but now these Sunday religious musings became longer, as if in preparation for his own death. He made several references to his will and worked hard on his accounts in the hope that he would leave no unpaid debts when he died (5/31/78).

On his sixty-seventh birthday Adams complained of his physical fatigue and failing memory (8/18/74). And when a week later he began a new diary volume, he feared his record would become "a monotonous record of insignificant events." Adams wrote on in the conviction that "the habit has become so fixed in me that I could scarcely discontinue it without materially disturbing my mind and perhaps increasing that tendency to indifference about all things around me which is already far too great" (10/26/74).

Even in the Centennial Year of the American Revolution Adams showed little enthusiasm for public activities, and in June, 1878, he began the thirty-first and last volume of his diary with the following pessimistic assessment of his prospects:

I enter upon this volume with mixed emotions. First a sense of the unutility which pervades my life, and next with a consciousness of the probability that it may be my last. Already whatever may be the anxieties that surround me, they carry with them nothing to make me sanguine of the future. I aspire to nothing and pray only that my condition be not extended for the worse. Thus far God has been abundant in his mercies. If it be his pleasure that I do not carry this record to its end—so be it I shall be content. (6/1/78)

After voting on election day of 1880, Adams found some confidence that despite the agitation between candidates and parties, the American system would survive, and this hopeful perception seemed to him to be "a proper place to terminate a Diary that has continued from the first of May in the year 1824 to this date fifty six years and six months." The last line in the diary is, "What I may do more I do not decide" (11/2/80).

Sidney George Fisher (1809–1871)

Although the extant portion of Fisher's diary spans thirty-six years, its first entry indicates that Fisher had engaged in at least one, if not several, other periods of journalizing, the last ending in the tragedy of his brother's death. The son of a socially prominent Philadelphia family, Fisher had the opportunity to encounter many of the most interesting and influential figures of the period. The very first surviving entry summarizes events of the previous year and includes an extremely long section on a trip to Washington during which time Fisher met with Senators John C. Calhoun, Henry Clay, and Daniel Webster and with President Jackson.[7]

These detailed and vivid portraits are only a few of the interesting character studies Fisher recorded in his diary. However, the essential focus was not on individuals but on a society. In recording the lives of the socially elite in Philadelphia, Fisher created an exceptional portrait of American society as seen from their point of view. The reader of the diary will find a fully preserved world. Describing balls and business manipulations, polite conversation and political scheming, Fisher portrayed events that, taken as a whole, chronicle the vast changes that were then taking place in American society—the financial panics that arose from wild speculation, the street riots against immigrants and abolitionists, and the coming of the age of steamships.

Fisher complained in the diary that society was much a "mystery" that no one could "really understand the might scene & vast movements around him . . . [or] pierce into the future or comprehend the past." He called history "a blind guide," arguing that "Nature never reproduces, never repeats itself. Each link in the wondrous chain of events differs from all which preceded it" (183). Yet, his own diary seems to dispute his assertion. For example, in an entry dated June 11, 1848, Fisher wrote prophetically, "The slavery question is becoming more important and more alarming every day. . . . new combinations will be formed, are forming, and there is great reason to fear that ere long there will be a Northern party and a Southern party and that the former . . . will attempt the entire abolition of slavery. This would be a signal for a civil war" (211).[8] Part of Fisher's distrust of history may have stemmed from his observation that the history of America had been and would be unlike that of Europe, and though he was confident that "it would be the theater of great events, of mighty developments of human power & action," he felt unable to determine whether it would become "the seat of a higher civilization, of a happier & purer life than the past" (163).

Fisher was aware that his diary was being pulled between personal concerns and his fascination with the vast social and political developments of mid-nineteenth century America:

I sometimes almost resolve to make my diary strictly personal and say nothing of public affairs, for if I noticed all and expressed about them what I thought and felt, I should do nothing but write what would be less a diary than a contemporaneous history of politics. But public events both from the great interests and great principles they involve, necessarily occupy much of the thought of anyone who thinks at all. (352)

One of the subjects that increasingly became a concern of the diary was the conflict that led to the Civil War; indeed, by the end of 1861 he could write that his diary had "become little else than a record of the events of the war" (407). Fisher had not always been hostile to the principle of slaveholding, but he became increasingly supportive of the abolitionist movement, even authoring books attacking the claims of slaveholders to legal and biblical sanctions for their positions. Fisher claimed in the diary that even the evidence he had received from associates whose "prejudices were all in favor of the system" showed *Uncle Tom's Cabin* was not inflammatory propaganda, but offered "a correct" if not a subdued portrait of "the enormities of slavery"; and that, if the full enormity of slavery were portrayed, "the description would be too horrible and revolting to read" (243).

In Fisher's, as in most diaries, the personal portrait is more important than any external one, and the most important theme in the diary is the almost tragic results of Fisher's patrician attitudes. I write "almost tragic," because Fisher never completely fell. He lost almost his entire fortune and labored under increasing debts, but generous "loans" from friends kept him from real poverty. Fisher's flaw was pride that kept him from making practical compromises that might have improved his fortunes. He did so even though his loss of wealth constantly forced him to endure more degrading situations. The very passivity of his life, which allowed him to observe the actions of others and thus contributed much to the effectiveness of his diary, kept him from effective action of his own.

Early in his life Fisher searched for direction. Educated for the law, he early determined not to practice because he felt that the profession seemed "calculated to narrow the mind, degrade the feelings and blunt the moral susceptibilities."[9] In some entries he considered the possibility that his time might "be more pleasantly employed in reading and society" or devoted "to such occupations as are suited to . . . [his] own tastes and intellectual bias," but he could find no better life (16). Although he looked with growing disgust at young lawyers "cringing" and "crawling" before established attorneys or prospective clients who might cast business their way, he ultimately concluded that the law was no different than other careers: "The professions . . . [had] become mere money making pursuits, business . . . [was] degrading & public life, disreputable." In his view no career was "satisfactory to a mind in any degree elevated above the common level," but life "without object" seemed equally worthy of condemnation. He wrote: "I cannot describe the strange feeling of unreality which I experience in my contemplation of existence. . . . Mine is the fatal gift of imagination . . . and all my life . . . has been dreaming, which leads to nothing instead of acting, by which I might frequently have accomplished much" (21, 29–30).

Fisher felt that his wealth, which made him "independent, tho not rich," would keep him from having to bother with activities that he considered beneath him (16, 21). He derived much of his income from a farm which he owned but did not work himself; however, by the end of 1843 the income that only two years earlier had been adequate had dropped by a third. The difference, Fisher realized, would have to "be made up by work," but he could not bring himself to do it. He protested in the diary that "the idea of being obliged to work is horrible . . . & involves an abandonment of my cherished tastes & the bias of my mind. . . . I detest business in all its forms, and am unfit to mix in the stir & struggles of the world" (147). In this regard he almost seems a prototype for Harold Skimpole in Charles Dickens's *Bleak House.*

As his life progressed, Fisher's failure to act ceased to be simply a concern about personal fulfillment and began to have significant consequences for his life-style. On his fifty-second birthday (March 2, 1861) he was mortified to have to admit, "I have done so little. I have wasted time, talents and money, all which, well employed, would have placed me in a very different position from that which I occupy." He refused to totally reject his past decisions or give up hope for the future. Instead, he insisted, "I have had so far on the whole a happy life and I trust, in what may be left, in some measure to retrieve the past" (380). Even with his fifty-eighth birthday approaching and illness impeding his ability to think, Fisher could still hope "to do some work which, if it have no other results, will give me the satisfactory sense of doing something, and of living for and with a worthy purpose" (523). Only toward the end of his life did Fisher "in sadness confess" that his diary had become a record of "a far from happy life." He admitted, "Advancing years, ill health, and poverty, a daily swarm of teasing, fretting anxieties & small hope of anything better in the future leave but little room for enjoyment" (558).

Modern readers may have little sympathy for Fisher, not only because his fall stemmed so directly from his own prideful disdain for work, but because, even after his circumstances had reduced him to living off the charity of his friends and relatives, he continued to claim his own superiority. He was upset that his wife had to engage in a "disgusting business . . . unfit for a lady," that of going in person to an employment office not to seek work, but to hire servants from "a crowd of hideous Irish monsters," few of whom, he believed, were "fit to enter a decent house" (558).

Fisher's prejudice extended not only to the Irish, but to all people whom he considered beneath his station. His standards were not based on wealth or occupation because such things might be achieved through effort by those with no hereditary claim to social position. Fisher believed that the members of Philadelphia society had "an air of refinement, dignity & simplicity of manner" because, unlike New York society which admitted the rich and powerful, it accepted "few whose families have not held the same station for several generations" (21). Fisher asserted that, "shy of a parvenu," his circle looked "sharply at a man's pretensions" (147).

If Fisher can be taken as a fair example of his social group, the standards of that circle were very restrictive. When a woman in his circle "married a man who had been a surgeon," Fisher concluded she could not have married for love because there could be "no congeniality or sympathy between them." Although the man had been "successful in his profession, [and] for a time indeed at the head of it," in Fisher's view the doctor was only "a vulgar man, with talents, but a common-place limited mind & no culture either as a gentleman or a scholar." Admitting that this doctor might be "a respectable person," Fisher snobbishly assumed that "a man whose life has been devoted to a me-chanical pursuit like surgery in which dexterity of manipulation is the chief merit and object, is not likely to possess superior tastes and en-largement of mind" (183). In another entry Fisher gave as his reason for breaking with one of his close friends: "His marriage and associa-tions which are in a sphere entirely different from mine will necessarily put an end to our intimacy" (69).

Fisher, himself, did not marry until he was in his forties because, while Elizabeth Ingersol, the woman he loved, was very much within his social circle, he knew that her marriage settlement would be small. A year and a half before his marriage Fisher wrote of his intention to make his diary "a record of events & thoughts, not of feelings," in order to move his life "from the influence of the heart into the domain of the mind," rather than alter his carefree life:

Now, as heretofore, love is within my reach. A word might change my des-tiny, and I *ought* to speak it, to have spoken it long ago. But want of courage to face the necessity of a life of labor which would instantly arise, a love of independence and freedom from care & imperative duties, of ease & reverie, of a contemplative unfettered life, inactive except from choice & not from permanent obligation, these hold me back. (231)

Despite these concerns, on May 28, 1851, Fisher married Elizabeth.

After his marriage Fisher went to live with his in-laws. His life at this point, as the following excerpts from the diary indicate, was a very comfortable one:

> Breakfast at 8, simply tea & toast or bread and butter—excellent both . . . the best in town—the table well served, a snowy cloth, nice china & silver, of which for poor people we have in good supply. . . . Thro the morning I read law, write letters, settle accounts, prepare cases, &c., till one or two o'clock, unless obliged to go out sooner. Then a walk with Bet. . . . The Atheneum till 5. Then dinner, always a good one, with 2 or 3 glasses of wine . . . the table well served and Elias nicely dressed—I hate an ill dressed slovenly waiter—a little talk with Bet after dinner, then cigars and a book— *not* a law book—till 8, when I am summoned to the parlor to tea. . . . So pass the days in calm happiness. (241)

As such entries suggest, Fisher did try to work as a lawyer; but, perhaps because of some feature of his character, he was never really successful. For example, his first opportunity to argue a case before the Supreme Court was "a decided failure." He "became embarrassed and lost presence of mind in speaking" (245). Neither this unsuccessful law practice, his farm, nor his books produced sufficient income to keep Fisher from going further into debt. His health declined along with his fortunes until his death in 1871.

As he felt his life drawing to a close, Fisher found his diary keeping becoming more, not less, important: "Even of my uneventful life I find much to say. As time advances, experience, study and reflection increase the material of thought, views enlarge, the world reveals new and manifold meanings and everything around me inspires a deeper interest as . . . [death] approaches. Some complain life is dull. I find it full of novelty and enjoyment, tho my path is excluded from business or society" (332). Even when ill health forced him to give up regular entries, Fisher still tried to maintain some record.[10]

Fisher kept his diary from more than habit. At various points in his life he had allowed the diary to lapse, only to decide to resume it. He was interested in the possibilities and limitations of the diary form:

> How little of a day, of its thoughts & feelings can be put in one diary. I would take a volume and then, if the actual truth were written down, one would wish to burn it. Whenever, under the excitement of reflection, I am tempted to write all that I feel on topics that produce emotion I find that either sen-

timent is too much colored by passion or that I do not want the truth to remain on record for others, perhaps, to read, & I tear it out. (318)

More than once Fisher wrote of rereading early entries and destroying those containing material that he did not want others to read after his death (306). Fortunately, most of the diary appears to have survived.

George Templeton Strong (1820–1875)

A comparison between the diaries of Fisher and Strong is almost unavoidable, if for no other reason than that their lives had significant similarities. Each man was a lawyer (each even argued a case before the Supreme Court); each was well connected in the society of his native city (Fisher in Philadelphia and Strong in New York); each seemed to know or know of everybody of importance; and each kept a diary over a long period of time.[11] As a result of these similarities we should not be surprised that each of their diaries holds a valuable portrait of life in its period.

However, there are significant differences between these men and their records. One difference has to do with the writers' comments on the diary form. Unlike Fisher, Strong rarely commented on the process of the diary keeping. Although in one entry Strong wrote that the "prototype" for his diary was Pepys's (a statement which shows that he was conscious of the diary as a literary form), he did not indicate which characteristics he sought to emulate.[12] Also unlike Fisher, Strong did not record any concern about the use of his diary by himself or others. Perhaps one reason for this lack of concern was that Strong created a far less personal document than did Fisher. Strong included some personal events, but those he felt most intensely, such as his estrangement from his son, were either "obliterated from the diary," or never recorded (4:558n).

Strong recorded comparatively little information about his relations. The most conspicuous exceptions to this practice were entries on those situations in which his relations had become involved in matters that had attracted public notice, such as the scandalous divorce trial of one of his cousins, or entries on incidents that were representative of some wider problem in his society, such as his father-in-law's financial crisis (2:53–58). Strong wrote about the latter incident not as a family matter, but as further evidence of the broader dangers of financial speculation: "People who are gentle and generous in every other relation of life are converted into harpies and devils when their dealings relate to debtor and creditor accounts. God preserve me from owing money! . . . What a miserable lesson this miserable business is against speculation" (2:45).

Strong was very clear in presenting his views on public issues, and the reader can make some assessments of his personality, but his vision was more consistently focused outward than that of most diarists. He recorded accounts of numerous events and the public reaction to them. Significantly, he not only recorded major historical events such as John Brown's raid and the death of Lincoln, but he also wrote about events that, though forgotten today, often give a better portrait of life in the period than more prominent ones. For example, he tells about the disastrous fire on the steamboat *Henry Clay* that resulted from a reckless race by two captains each eager to prove the superiority of his ship (2:102–103). In other sections of the diary he describes such events as the "Quarantine War," in which mobs, claiming to be protesting the danger of infection but really fearing that the value of their property would suffer, burned down hospitals and tossed their smallpox and yellow fever patients out in the cold (2:412), and the opening of Madison Avenue in midtown Manhattan, a street now synonymous with the advertising industry, but then "a rough and ragged track . . . rich in mudholes, goats, pigs, geese, and stramonium. Here and there Irish shanties 'come out' (like smallpox pustules), each composed of a dozen rotten boards and a piece of stove pipe for a chimney" (4:155).

Even when he recorded an event that is still famous, Strong frequently included details that give the reader a special perspective on it. In writing about the Chicago Fire, he emphasized how the event showed the interconnection of widely separated parts of the country by noting that because wealthy New Yorkers had investments in Chicago, the fire threatened charitable subscriptions for an orchestra: "Strange there should be a connection of cause and effect between a kerosene lamp kicked over in a Chicago cow stable and the performance of Haydn's and Beethoven's church music in New York—that a careless boy should thus paralyze our orchestra and chorus" (4:390–92).

On a few occasions Strong was so touched by the scenes he observed that he lost his detachment, demonstrating that he was capable of deep feeling. How appropriate was it, he wondered, for Northern philanthropists to be "scolding" about slavery in the South while in New York "swarms of seamstresses . . . [were forced to] toil in monotonous drudgery" for bare subsistence; and while one couldn't "walk the length of Broadway without meeting some hideous troop of ragged girls from twelve years old down, brutalized already beyond redemption by premature vice, clad in the filthy refuse of the rag-pickers collections, obscene of speech the stamp of childhood gone from their faces, hurrying along with harsh laughter and foulness on their lips that some have learned by rote, yet too young to understand it; with thief written in their cunning eyes and whore on their depraved faces" (2:56–57).

In this entry as in many others Strong offered observations that show that his world is not as far removed from our own as it may seem and that his portrayal may help us to look at our own world in a new way. For example, his description of the reaction to the arrival of Jenny Lind shows that the frenzied adoration of musical performers is not unique to the twentieth century: "Jenny Lind has arrived, and was received with such a spontaneous outbreak of rushing and crowding, and hurrahing, and serenading as this city has never seen before . . . horses [were] hardly permitted to carry her through the streets, so vehemently did the mob thirst for the honor of drawing her carriage" (2:17–18). Calling this fanaticism "Lindomania," Strong compared it to "lycanthropy" in its power to make humans act like animals: "It's a morbid passion for assuming the form of an ass and paying six dollars and so on for the privilege of drinking in her most sweet voice through the preternaturally prolonged ears of the victims of this terrible new disorder" (2:21). However, even Strong proved not to be totally immune from the disease and went to hear Lind sing.

Strong viewed and recorded a number of the fads and fashions of the period, such as water cures and spiritualism. He satirized the proponents of the spirit-rapping fad who had begun publishing what they claimed were "communications" from beyond the grave, including pronouncements "from George Washington, Jefferson, Andrew Jackson, Margaret Fuller, and a great many other people," noting that "all of them [were] writing very remarkably alike, and most of them [with] very questionable grammar" (2:93). Strong even attended some of the lecture-discussions that the Transcendentalist Bronson Alcott called his "Conversations" (2:300–301).

A good portion of Strong's diary deals with the events relating to the Civil War. In 1856 he became a member and an ardent supporter of the Republican party. In the entries of this period he maintained that, while in the abstract slavery did not violate "moral law," the practice of "slavery as it *exists* at the South . . . is the greatest crime on the largest scale known in modern history . . . [being] intended to extinguish and annihilate the moral being of men for profit; systematic murder not of the physical, but of the moral and intellectual being" (2:304–5). He was not initially for forced abolition, for while he argued that "slavery demoralizes and degrades the community in which it exists," and so should be prohibited in the unsettled territories, he still believed that outsiders should not be allowed to interfere with it in states where it was already established (2:287–88). He argued that his own sentiments and those of many Northerners had an economic origin, that Southern efforts in the 1850s to extend slavery into new territories "taught us that the two systems could not co-exist in the same territory . . . and that if we allowed slaves to enter any territorial acquisition, our own free labor must be excluded from it" (3:67).

Strong expressed dismay at the weak stand of Buchanan: "The Old Pennsylvania Fossil is rumored to have lapsed into vacillation and imbecility. It seemed a week ago as if he were developing germs of a backbone. Had this old mollusk become vertebrate, the theories of Darwin . . . would have been confirmed" (3:89). And while not originally a supporter of Lincoln, he soon began to praise him. Given the opportunity to enjoy "an hour's free and easy talk" with the president, Strong concluded, "He is a barbarian, Scythian, yahoo, or gorilla, in respect of outside polish . . . but a most sensible, straightforward, honest old codger. The best President we have had since old Jackson's time" (3:204–5).

But Strong's enthusiasm for Lincoln was not continuous, and the diary preserves his shifting sentiments. By the fall of 1862 Strong became concerned about repeated Union failures. Hearing that many Northern regiments were worn, demoralized, and undisciplined, he began to write of rumors of a military coup in which Southern and Union generals would "all come together and agree on some compromise or adjustment, turn out Lincoln and his 'Black Republicans' and use their respective armies to enforce their decision North and South and reestablish the Union" (3:255–56). Strong wrote, "Even Lincoln has gone down at last. . . . This honest old codger was the last to fall, but he has fallen. Nobody believes him any more. I do not, though I still maintain him. . . . But it is impossible to resist the conviction that he is unequal to his place. His only special gift is fertility of smutty stories." He ended the entry "Oh Abraham, O mon Roi!" (3:256). But a year later Union victories had once more made Strong optimistic.

Strong's accounts of the war itself, though well written, were second- or third-hand and less interesting than the personalized history in passages like those above dealing with Lincoln, those dealing with the draft riots of 1863 in his own city, or reaction to the news that Richmond had fallen:

An enormous crowd soon blocked that part of Wall Street and speeches began. . . . Never before did I hear cheering that came straight from the heart, that was given because the people felt relieved by cheering and hallooing. All the cheers I ever listened to were tame in comparison, because seemingly inspired only by a design to show enthusiasm. These were spontaneous and involuntary and of vast "magnetizing" power. They sang . . . "The Star-Spangled Banner," repeating the last two lines of Key's song over and over. . . .

I walked about on the outskirts of the crowd, shaking hands with everybody, congratulating and being congratulated by scores of men I hardly know even by sight. Men embraced and hugged each other, *kissed* each other, retreated into doorways to dry their eyes and came out again to flourish their hats and hurrah. (3:574–75)

Believing that the South was responsible for starting the war and, therefore, for the destruction it caused, Strong endorsed a strict policy toward the defeated states of the Confederacy: "The South is crushed for a time, but the more bitter and vindictive for its humiliation, and fuller than ever, even of sectional, anti-national, traitorous impulses. Nothing but physical exhaustion keeps the Southern Hyena from instantly flying at our throats" (4:64).

Yet even the war and reconstruction never dominated the diary. It is full of too many subjects, such as the political manipulations of Boss Tweed and the financial schemes of James Fisk and Jay Gould. Another of the most frequent subjects in Strong's diary is Columbia University. For many years Strong served conscientiously as one of its trustees; yet, none of the obligations he assumed in that role was more faithfully kept than that which he kept to his diary. He wrote until June 25, 1875; he died on July 21.

Chapter Eight
Transcendentalist Journals

Transcendentalism began as part of the romantic movement's opposition to the Age of Reason.[1] The Transcendentalists rejected the materialistic position promulgated by the British philosopher John Locke, that all knowledge comes through the senses, in favor of that of the German philosopher Immanuel Kant, who claimed that there were certain ideas innate to the mind, Furthermore, they questioned the very reality of the world that was perceived through the senses, believing instead that the real world was spiritual and could only be recognized by some process that transcended physical appearances.

Such a philosophy would seem to discourage interest in the physical world, including the study of nature and social reform; but, paradoxically, the reverse proved to be true. In *Nature,* the work which established his reputation, Emerson, the most influential of the American Transcendentalists, defined "Nature" as the physical world and stressed that the spiritual was more valuable than the physical. However, he insisted that he had "no hostility to nature, but a child's love to it." Nature, he contended, was of great value as a symbolic representation of spiritual reality, and as such it could teach man to transcend physical appearance. His disciples, including Henry David Thoreau and John Burroughs, were among the best-known nature writers of their times. Their diaries, which are considered in this chapter, were to a great extent devoted to the love and study of physical nature. They did attempt to use their studies of nature to develop perceptions about the spiritual world, but the reader of their diaries might almost conclude that they found physical nature enough.

Emerson has been severely criticized for his lack of involvement in the reform movements of his day; however, other Transcendentalists were among the leaders in many of these movements. Thoreau is famous for his opposition to slavery and his efforts in refining Bronson Alcott's concept of civil disobedience. His cabin at Walden Pond was a station of the underground railroad that smuggled fugitive slaves toward Canada. Another diarist treated in this chapter, Thomas Went-

worth Higginson, was also famous for his involvement in the abolitionist movement.

Though the diaries covered in this chapter seem more concerned
with the physical world than those of Emerson and Alcott, they were
all rooted in a concern for higher principles. They show that the building of a cabin at Walden Pond or work in some social cause can advance
the principles of Transcendentalism. These writers widen the application of Transcendentalism and help to assure its influence in our own
era.

Henry David Thoreau (1817–1862)

Few American authors are so clearly associated with the repudiation
of material possessions as is Henry David Thoreau; and, therefore, it
seems ironic that the thirty-nine volumes of Thoreau's journal should
have finally come into the possession of J. Pierpont Morgan, a man
associated with the accumulation of material wealth. Yet, thanks to
Morgan's bequest, these volumes and the wooden box which Thoreau
himself crafted for them have been preserved for scholarship in the J.
Pierpont Morgan Library in New York City.

These volumes usually occupied a position between Thoreau's initial
notes and his public works. Thoreau was never without his notebook
for, believing that "impulse" was "the best linguist" and the "most
convincing" logician, he worried that a cool analysis might threaten
his inspiration.[2] Such analysis was important to his work, but he determined to leave it for a later stage of composition that would occur
when he had the opportunity to copy a few lines from his notebook
into an expanded journal entry. So extensive was this expansion that a
notebook entry which took "but five minutes to write in the field"
might fill several pages in the journal.[3]

The fact that Thoreau revised his entries in adapting them for his
published works has been one argument for downgrading their importance. In one of the earliest published studies of the *Journal*, Paul Elmer More rejected their claim to any intrinsic merit: "The bulk of these
note-books have no interest except for the confirmed nature worshiper,
and . . . little even for him. Most of the memorable reflections and
descriptive passages had already been transferred to the regular books
and lectures; what remains is made up largely of trivial daily memo-
randa." More admitted that the work contained "isolated examples of
wit and poetry," but he maintained that their only significant value

was to corroborate Thoreau's sincerity in his published writing.[4]

In a similar manner Thoreau himself was once dismissed as the mere "shadow" of Emerson. However, just as Thoreau has come to be regarded as an original thinker, so his *Journal* has increasingly become recognized as important not just for its insights into other writings such as *Walden,* but as an intrinsically valuable piece of writing. The editors of the new standard edition of the *Journal* were not taking a new or particularly extreme position when they called it "the major written work of Thoreau's life" (1:592). In his introduction to *The Heart of Thoreau's Journals,* published in 1927, Odell Shepard claimed that Thoreau's public writings, even *Walden* are examples of his "talent," but the *Journals* are "products of his genius."[5] In 1958 Perry Miller had gone so far as to suggest that the journal was "a deliberate work of art, in no respect subsidiary to the artist's public appearances," an art work so impressive that it might, to a significant extent, account for the fact that "Thoreau's reputation has expanded almost beyond recognition since the publication of the *Journal* in 1906."[6] In 1960 Laurence Stapleton called it "Thoreau's principal if not his greatest work."[7] And most recently Sharon Cameron in *Writing Nature* emphasized that "Thoreau came to think of the *Journal* as his central literary enterprise."[8]

Most of Thoreau's earliest journals were destroyed, some while being revised into various public productions. Fortunately, Thoreau copied much of this material into other volumes. The earliest of these volumes bearing the legend, "Gleanings–Or What Time Has Not Reaped of My Journal" is a copy of an 1837 diary.[9] The first entry in the extant portion of the *Journal* (after quotations from Herbert, Burton, and Marvell) begins: "Oct 22nd 1837 'What are you doing now?' he asked, 'Do you keep a journal?'—So I make my first entry to-day." This line almost certainly refers to Emerson, just as the following lines ("Solitude—To be alone I find it necessary to escape the present—I avoid myself." [10/22/37]) were adapted from Emerson's *Nature.* However, while Emerson served as the inspiration for Thoreau's mature journalizing, Thoreau had previously kept serial records. While in college he kept both a commonplace book which he titled "Miscellaneous Extracts" and an "Index rerum" comprised of "extracts from his reading . . . book reviews . . . and reading lists."[10] As early as 1835 Thoreau, in a college essay, argued for the value of such notebooks: "as those pieces which the painter sketches for his own amusement in his leisure hours, are often superior to his most elaborate productions, so it is that ideas often suggest themselves to us spontaneously, as it were, far surpassing in beauty those which arise in the mind upon applying ourselves to any particular subject." In this essay, written more than two years before his first journal entry, Thoreau declared the inadequacy of such raw notes, arguing that the major value in preserving such "scattered thoughts" depends on the journalist's ability to express them to others. Thus even before his first entry Thoreau saw diary keeping as a step toward the development of public works.[11]

Some scholars have suggested with differing degrees of emphasis that an important, although never fully realized, function of the journal was to create "a 'Kalendar' or 'Atlas' of Concord,'" a belief held by Bronson Alcott, who had used his own journals in a similar way in the creation of his book *Concord Days*. Stapleton accepted a similar idea, arguing that "the latter volumes of his [Thoreau's] *Journal* are full of raw material for his book on Concord—a Concord mythology . . . [containing] everything about the inhabitants—from human beings to frogs."[12]

This conception of the journals as an incomplete version of Thoreau's intentions has led some scholars to conclude that they are inferior to the public works; however, as we have already seen, this view is not generally accepted. Indeed, one of the particular values of diary literature is in preserving a process of pursuing an evolving truth rather than in establishing an unchanging one. This view is particularly suited to a consideration of Thoreau, who believed with Emerson that the process was more important than the product, and who asserted the cyclical pattern of existence. Thoreau did not claim to have found final answers. Readers who try to approach *Walden* with the idea that Thoreau was trying to describe the ideal society are mistaken and ignore Thoreau's own admission in it that he had left Walden to pursue other experiments. The journal by its very nature supports Thoreau's values.

Early in his journal Thoreau expressed the concern that, while each day had something to teach him, he might at the time "lack the discernment to distinguish the whole lesson" (11/12/37). Though he hoped that his diary might keep that lesson from being lost, Thoreau was not always confident that it would yield useful material. He worried that the moment of inspiration might pass too quickly to allow his ideas to be preserved (6/26/40). He even questioned, "But what does all this scribbling amount to?" speculating that what was "scribbled in the heat moment" might later seem without value, the "shell" of what had earlier seemed alive and vital (3/5/38). Later, as Thoreau became more confident about his journalizing, these concerns lessened.

Many diarists include in their record comments on their intentions and attitudes toward their diaries, but few as frequently or as articulately as Thoreau, who seems extremely conscious of his practice. Perhaps the most eloquent and telling of these comments was made on February 8, 1841:

My Journal is that of me which would else spill over and run to waste.— gleanings from the field which in action I reap. I must not live for it, but in it for the gods—They are my correspondent to whom daily I send off this sheet post paid. I am clerk in their counting room and at evening transfer the account from day-book to ledger.

The mystical communication made possible by the journals was bidirectional. Thoreau would use them not only as a means of expressing his soul to the gods, but also as a means of deciphering their communications to him. In one entry he tells of how, while on a walk to hunt for arrowheads, he had begun a reverie on the Indians who once inhabited the region. After concluding his speech with "Here . . . stood Tahatawan and there . . . is Tahatawan's arrowhead," he dug up the "ordinary stone which . . . [his] whim had selected," and found it to be, "a most perfect arrowhead, as sharp as if just from the hands of the Indian fabricator" (10/29/37). This incident may serve as a model for Thoreau's method of composition in the *Journal;* after immersing himself in his materials, he would yield to the reveries of the journal. Then looking over what had seemed to come forth so casually and without planning, he would find shape, order, and purpose, just as if his fantasy had been guided by some mystical force. As the journal form preserves the order of and attempts to be a faithful rendering of the divine communication through Nature, it offered Thoreau a superior opportunity to see and express truth: "Thoughts accidentally thrown together become a frame in which more may be developed and exhibited. Perhaps this is the main value of the habit of writing, of keeping a journal— that so we remember our best hours and stimulate ourselves" (1/22/52).

At the end of one long entry Thoreau expressed his belief that a journal might be superior to the reorganization of its materials into a more self-consciously contrived art form:

I do not know but thoughts written down thus in a journal might be printed in the same form with greater advantage than if the related ones were brought together into separate essays. They are now allied to life, and are seen by the reader not to be far-fetched. It is more simple, less artful. I feel that in the other case I should have no proper frame for my sketches. (1/27/52)

Fortunately such concerns did not finally hinder him from adapting diary material. Most of Thoreau's public writings, including *Walden,* had their origins in his journal. These writings were not merely revisions of journal sections, but more complex reworkings of journal material. The process by which Thoreau transformed the journal into *Walden* was far from simple.[13] Let us consider one of the most famous passages in *Walden*:

If a man does not keep pace with his companions, perhaps it is because he hears a different drummer. Let him step to the music he hears however measured or far away.[14]

This passage seems to have been developed from a series of journal entries rather than a single one. Both of the following journal excerpts contain elements that lead to the production of the version in *Walden*:

A man's life should be a stately march to a sweet but unheard music, and when to his fellows it shall seem irregular and unharmonious, he will only be stepping to a livelier measure. (6/30/40)

Let a man step to the music he hears, however measured. (7/19/51)

In language and imagery these excerpts echo that in the public work. However, all uses of diary material are not always so obvious. Consider a third excerpt:

It is not so much the music as the marching to the music that I feel. (9/7/51)

This passage is not as clearly related to the version in *Walden* as are the other two, but its relation to the earlier entries suggest that it was part of the process by which Thoreau developed the public version.[15]

While all except the most ardent admirers of the *Journal* would agree that *Walden* is a greater work of art than its component passages in the *Journal,*[16] even in isolation an original entry may have advantages over version that appears in *Walden,* if only because its use and context in the latter required the alteration or deletion of a worthy idea or expression:

Journal:
I find an instinct in me conducting to a mystic spiritual life, and also another to a primitive savage life.

Toward evening, as the world waxes darker, I am permitted to see the woodchuck stealing across my path and am tempted to seize and devour it raw. (8/23/45)

Walden:
As I came home through the woods . . . it being now quite dark, I caught a glimpse of a woodchuck stealing across my path, and felt a strange thrill of savage delight, and was strongly tempted to seize and devour him raw. . . . I find in myself, and still find, an instinct toward a higher, or, as it is named, spiritual life as do most men, and another toward a primitive rank and savage one, and I reverence them both. (210)

In the passage from *Walden* the darkness Thoreau mentions seems purely physical, and there is nothing to temper the usual assumption that the lack of light impeded his ability to see the woodchuck. The passage also seems to indicate that Thoreau's temptation to devour the woodchuck was an internal one. In the journal entry the sinister associations with darkness seem more viable. His ability to see the woodchuck was "permitted" as if willed by some external power, and the structure of the sentence makes Thoreau's temptation seem similarly directed. In the journal entry the reader can see that Thoreau's love for "the wild" may include darker impulses than those he saw fit to reveal in *Walden.*

For Thoreau even the most casual observation might be important to mystical communication. "Mere facts and names and dates" might "communicate more than we suspect," just as a flower might not look as well "in the nosegay" as "in the meadow where it grew" (1/27/52). However, in praising the value of such details in a journal, Thoreau was not suggesting that their use should be equally material. Declaring "the actual" to be "far less real . . . than the imagined," he feared that a diary of events would be but "a journal of the winds that blew while we were here." Just as he saw "thoughts" as "the epochs of our life," so he hoped to make his journal one of thoughts (6-/50). This is not to say that his diary lacks descriptions of the physical world. Indeed, for long stretches the recording of such material observations seems to be the primary function of the work; however, Thoreau kept returning to the principle that the main reason for recording such material facts was so that they might serve to develop the spiritual truths they symbolized: "Be greedy of occasions to express your thought. Improve the opportunity to draw analogies" (9/4/51).

Such analogies between sensory observations and the truths they represent might not be immediately apparent, and so one function of the journal was to preserve observations so that they might be used later. Thoreau wrote that, "Of all the strange and unaccountable-things this journalizing is the strangest. . . . If I make a huge effort to expose my innermost and richest wares to light, my counter seems cluttered with the meanest homemade stuffs, but after months or years, I may discover the wealth of India . . . and what perhaps seemed a festoon of dried apple or pumpkin will prove a string of Brazilian diamonds, or pearls from Corromandel" (1/29/41).

In some parts of his journal Thoreau seems very much the scientific naturalist. Asserting that "science is always brave, for to know is good," Thoreau sought to record even the meanest facts of his world (12/39). He held a certain fondness for data. Just as in *Walden* he recorded his expenditures to the fraction of a cent, so in his journal he preserved details. For example, one of his entries includes several columns of figures in which he recorded his raw and averaged measurements of the snow-cover; in other entries he gave an item-by-item analysis of the content of various birds' nests (1/12/56, 1/18/56 & 1/20/56). Many of his entries are accompanied by simple but skillful illustrations of the shape of a leaf or the patterns of animal tracks in the snow.

Thoreau appears to have had both skill and interest in such observations, but sometimes he found it necessary to remind himself that this tendency toward objective detachment might be drawing him away from the proper uses of its study: "Man cannot afford to be a naturalist, to look at Nature directly, but only with the side of his eye. he must look through her and beyond her. To look at her is as fatal as to look at the head of Medusa. It turns the man of science to stone. I feel I am dissipated by so many observations" (3/23/53). The warning would not have been necessary if Thoreau had not felt the fatal attraction of the material world. While natural forms were a delight, they might become an end in themselves leading the observer away from what Thoreau considered "true knowledge" and toward the "inhumanity of science." Such a warning is called forth in one entry in which he wrote about being "tempted to kill a rare snake that I may ascertain his species" (5/28/54).

Thoreau sought to study all the "moods and manners" of Nature, regarding even the crudest facts as important. He sought the wild, wanting "something speaking in measure to the condition of muskrats and skunk-cabbage"; indeed, he declared, "primitive nature is the most interesting to me" (11/16/50). Heeding Emerson's warning in "The American Scholar" that "So much of nature as [one] . . . is ignorant of, so much of his own mind does he not possess," Thoreau strove in his pursuit of the ideal to learn all he could of the material. Spiritual and physical, heaven and earth were halves of the same whole, a unified "poem" created by God. By recording all the phenomena of his world in the pages of his journal, he hoped to make them a transcription of that artwork. To his dismay he found that he did not have "the entire poem," but only an imperfect copy, for, even in the middle of the nineteenth century, it was obvious that the early settlers and their descendants had "torn out many of the first leaves and grandest passages." Considering that the larger, "nobler animals . . . [had] been exterminated," he lamented, "Is it not a maimed and imperfect nature that I am conversant with? As if I were to study a tribe of Indians that had lost all its warriors" (3/23/56).

But even if nature had been whole it would have proven insufficient for Thoreau's real needs. Early in the journal he warns that "the facts of science may dust the mind by their dryness, unless they are in a sense effaced each morning or rather rendered fertile by the dews of fresh and living truth" (7/7/51). Without some way to relate a scientific fact to some spiritual principle, the fact might not only be valueless, but actually harmful to the mission of the soul. Therefore, although Thoreau felt drawn to the role of scientific naturalist, he fought that tendency. The journal shows him repeatedly rediscovering the principle that "there is no such thing as pure *objective* observation. Your observation to be interesting, *i.e.* to be significant, must be *subjective*. . . . The man of most science is the man most alive, whose life is the greatest event. Senses that take cognizance of outward things merely are of no avail" (5/6/54). Even when his subject is the wonders of nature, Thoreau finds objective observation unsatisfying. Nature, he declares, "excites an expectation which she cannot satisfy. The merest child which has rambled into a copsewood dreams of a wilderness so wild and strange and inexhaustible as Nature can never show him" (5/23/54). For Thoreau, the very wonders of nature teach man that he must go beyond science.

Although, as Thoreau himself knew, he was "by constitution as good an observer" as the traditional scientists, most of the scientific community could not understand his attitude toward the sciences. Many, if not most, would have considered it a contradiction in terms to claim, as Thoreau did, to be simultaneously "a mystic, a transcendentalist, and a natural philosopher" (3/5/53). Perhaps part of this complex position resulted from the vastness of Thoreau's interests. He declared an "affection for any aspect of the world," explaining "I have no more distinctness or pointedness in my yearnings than an expanding bud, which does indeed point to flower and fruit, to summer and autumn, but is aware of the warm sun and spring influence only" (11/16/50). His journal entries are so varied in their content because the whole universe drew his interest and love.

Possibly as a result of his attempt to embrace these different interests, Thoreau seems to have been constantly shifting his views about what constituted the appropriate content of a diary; but perhaps it is more fitting to say that his views were so complex that they embraced some apparent contradictions. In some entries Thoreau declared that his journal should record only "the things I love" and that it should be "a record of the mellow ripe moments" preserving the "kernal" rather than "the husk of life" (11/16/50 & 12/22/51). In other entries he wrote what seems a very different message, one that suggests that a journal must not neglect even seemingly trivial external facts, for they could have a profound effect on our lives: "In a journal it is important in a few words to describe the weather, or character of the day as it affects our feelings. That which was so important at the time cannot be unimportant to remember" (2/5/55).

Like Emerson and Whitman, Thoreau showed little concern about such apparent contradictions among his assertions. Nowhere is this fact more apparent than in what seems his shifting valuation of the ideal and the material. In one entry he declares "I do not think much of the actual. It is something which we have long since done with. It is a sort of vomit in which the unclean love to wallow" (6-/50). In another, he argues that without the physical, spiritual achievement would be impossible: "We cannot write well or truly but what we write with gusto. The body, the senses, must conspire with the mind. Expression must be the act of the whole man. . . . The intellect is powerless to express thought without the aid of the heart and liver and of every member" (9/2/51).

Part of the process of moving from objective observation to subjective "truth" involved the conversion of simple observation to imagery; the light reflected off a pond became transformed into "a dance of diamonds" and the squirrel's tails into "banners." On a slightly more complex level the beach sand suggested the hourglass of time which in turn inspired him to renew his dedication to life (11/8/51).

In attempting to discover some unifying pattern for Thoreau's journal, it would have been convenient to have found the same movement from lower to higher principles that he traced in *Walden;* however, if anything, the earlier entries seem more directed toward the abstract and the ideal than are the later ones. Perhaps a fitting description of the development of the journal is that the line between objective observation and subjective thought becomes less rigid as the diary progresses. Thoreau himself expressed the same idea in the journal, writing that he found some facts to be not only "quite above the level of the actual," but even beyond those of his philosophy. As a result, he concluded that "the boundaries of the actual are no more fixed and rigid than the elasticity of our imaginations." That "some incidents . . . seemed far more allegorical than actual," suggested to him that their real use was to convey that "allegorical significance" (5/31/53).

One such incident recorded in the journal illustrates the point:

The other day, as I stood on Walden, drinking at a puddle on the ice . . . I was amused to see an Irish laborer on the railroad, who had come down to drink, timidly tiptoeing toward me in his cowhide boots, lifting them nearly two feet at each step and fairly trembling with fear, as if the ice was already bending beneath his ponderous body and he were about to be engulfed. "Why man," I called out to him, "this ice will bear a loaded train." . . .

So, when I have been resting and quenching my thirst on the eternal plains of truth, where rests the base of those beautiful columns that sustain the heavens, I have been amused to find a traveler who had long confined himself to the quaking shore . . . come timidly tiptoeing toward me. (2/4/57)

Such an extraction of a spiritual from a real event is very much like practices that may be observed in the journals kept in New England by the Puritans a hundred years earlier.[17] Just as the Puritans believed that the examination of a divinely created world would show the ordering force of its creator, so Thoreau believed that the physical facts he recorded in his journal would reveal hidden truths.

Thoreau looked to some higher justification for the existence of suffering on earth, but the journal shows that he was not always the confident idealist of his public writings. He had periods of self-doubt, and used his journal to turn his concerns into a new confidence. For example, seven days after his thirty-fourth birthday Thoreau complained in his journal that he had made so little progress toward his "ideal" life that he felt "unborn." Considering that at his pace of development he would die before reaching maturity, Thoreau felt pressured to reduce his goals to make their achievement possible. However, as the entry developed he began to explore the possibility that, as life extends beyond the material world, he would have time to mature after aging and death have affected his physical existence: "This rapid revolution of nature, even of nature in me, why should it hurry me? . . . May not my life in nature, in proportion as it is supernatural, be only the spring and infantile portion of my spirit's life? . . . May I not sacrifice a hasty and petty completeness here to entireness there?" Finally, he concluded, "If life is a waiting, so be it. I will not be shipwrecked on a vain reality" (7/19/51).

It is significant that this announcement of a time scale beyond time appears in a diary entry with a fixed date. A study of the journal suggests that Thoreau did not so much march to the beat of "a different drummer" as to the beats of several drummers, choosing among them or, rather, merging them into a more complex rhythm than any might produce alone. The journal dates offer the rhythm of the sun's passage through the sky, the timing of the days and the seasons, but the contents reveal other scales less apparent to the physical senses.

Thoreau showed his ability to follow such different rhythms in his rearrangement of journal material into *Walden*. Just before the concluding chapter of *Walden* Thoreau wrote: "Thus was my first year's life in the woods completed; and the second was similar to it" (319). The statement seems to suggest that *Walden* was an account of only that first year; however, an examination of the journal shows conclusively that *Walden* was developed from entries written during both years' residence at the pond as well as from entries written before and after that residence. One purpose in this temporal "sleight of hand" was to allow the seasonal cycle to serve as a structural and symbolic device. Moreover, Thoreau did not simply reorder journal entries by season, he followed numerous symbolic patterns, moving skillfully among them.

Thoreau, like Whitman, determined that, in order to transcend the physical universe, it was "necessary to escape the present" (10/22/37). In "Passage to India" Whitman asserted that a man's existence in time and space was to "identify" him, to provide a stable base upon which he might "launch to those superior universes" that lay beyond time. The dating of Thoreau's journal entries serve a similar function; they identify but do not limit his thoughts and their relations to each other. In this sense Thoreau's journal achieved as much as any part of the physical universe can. Thoreau would probably have agreed that the words of a higher-order work must be written with the soul as well as with a pen. In his journal he used both instruments with great skill.

Thomas Wentworth Higginson (1823–1911)

Early in his career Thomas Wentworth Higginson was a disciple of Transcendentalism, and though he later distanced himself from the movement, he is properly associated with it. Like all of the American Transcendentalists Higginson was influenced by the abstract philosophy of Emerson, but he was increasingly more interested in the practical liberal reformism identified with William Henry Channing and Henry David Thoreau.

During his lifetime Higginson was highly regarded for his achievements as an author, editor, critic, and historian. But today most students of literature encounter Higginson only in references to other writers, especially Emily Dickinson.[18] He was also an acquaintance of Charlotte Forten and was often mentioned in her diary.[19] Higginson is still valued by scholars; Howard Mumford Jones called *Army Life in a Black Regiment*, fashioned from a portion of his journals, "a forgotten masterpiece."[20] Unfortunately, as of this writing, most of Higginson's diary record is only available in manuscript.[21]

The manuscripts of Higginson's personal record fall into two groups. The first group, which Higginson titled *Journals,* are generally composed of full and regular entries in ordinary lined or unlined copybooks. The last extant volume of these *Journals* was written in 1864. Higginson began another type of serial record in 1863 using books printed for use as datebooks or diaries. These volumes have dated pages or sections, and most have the year or the word *Diary* embossed on their covers. Unfortunately, with occasional exceptions, the entries are limited to brief notes. The *Journals* contain far more material related to internal and spiritual concerns than do the *Diaries;* however, they are still basically parts of the same life diary.

Higginson began his journals in 1835, when he was only twelve years old. His mother Louisa Higginson kept a diary, and her influence and example may have led Higginson to begin his record.[22] Edelstein in his biography of Higginson noted that although Higginson often wrote "about his mother, his father—as if he had never existed—remained relatively absent from his public statements." A notable exception is a diary entry written about four years after his father's death in 1834 in which Higginson claimed that he was "unfortunately too young at that time to feel . . . [that] loss very much."[23] One need not have a very great acquaintance with ten-year-old boys to be suspicious of such a statement and to wonder if that death and the dislocations it led to may have had an influence on the initiation of the diary. The diary also includes an incident in which Higginson, when a college student, tried to deal with depression by visiting his father's grave.[24]

Higginson, who was only fourteen when he entered Harvard, began a diary of his college years with his entrance examination: "At six in the morning we are all assembled at the south door. The names of the instructors and the number of those sent by each were taken down. . . . We were given English to be turned into Latin to do which about half the morning was allowed us, being called up at intervals to be examined. . . . I was asked the signification of a deponent verb" (8/29/37). A good portion of this first college diary concerns classes, exams, and grades, but Higginson showed that college life was not always centered about work. He mentions as well loafing, walks, and dances.

By the time he started the second volume of his journals Higginson had begun to show his competitiveness in the pursuit of academic standing, complaining that some of his grades were too low and boasting that another student "can't beat me without a struggle" (7/3/39, 5/22/39). Another of his interests in this portion of the journals was women. Indeed, the romance and courtship material in the early volumes are just one aspect of the diary's focus on its author's attempt to move from the role of dependent child to independent adult.[25]

Higginson's first love was Phebe Adam. In July, 1839 he wrote in his journal, "A little lonely—not very. Saw Phebe Adam . . . now a fine looking girl of sweet sixteen. I think I'll fall in love with her in vacation!" (7/11/39) There is no indication that this vacation romance ever occurred, but in the beginning of the next year he wrote that he had "had a glorious flirtation with Phebe" (1/31/40). Several passages of this section of the diary were removed, including one next to the words "decidedly smitten" (7/17/39).

However, the following summer his love left for Europe with her family, and Higginson realized that he had "looked on Phebe for the last time" (8/30/40). Determined to forget her if he could, Higginson bid good-bye in the journal. His words make it clear that this romance involved more thought than action or even talk: "Phebe Grant Adam— my first, best, sweetest loved one—the adoration which I have preserved untold, at first when I used to see you whether you smiled or frowned. I now for the many months that I have had no words from those beloved lips—this love stronger and deeper than man ever felt I for the last time express. . . . Phebe farewell" (8/31/40).

During vacations in the summer of 1840 and the winter of 1841 Higginson used separate small books to record travel diaries of two trips, the first to the White Mountains and the second to Virginia. The latter is important because it was Higginson's first trip to the slave states, and though he would later claim that such a brief exposure would be sufficient to convince one of the correctness of the abolitionist position, his record lacks any indication of this development.

Higginson graduated from Harvard in the summer of 1841, and that September began a new volume in his diary to record his new life as a schoolteacher. In its earliest entries he described himself on "a chilly September evening a quarter past nine . . . I am sitting in my new room having passed one day of my new life. I entered upon my new duties." He seems to have felt a certain mixture of pride and apprehension at finding himself "launched upon the world at last alone!" (9/18/41, 9/20/41). He soon gave up teaching to return to Harvard and eventually enrolled in the Divinity School. It was during this period that he began to read and become influenced by the Transcendentalists and supporters of social reform, especially the abolitionists. Unfortunately, there is a lapse in the extant diaries from the time shortly after he began his divinity school studies, the lapse coinciding with Higginson's engagement to Mary Channing, and the beginning of his career as a minister and a social reformer.

Then in 1949 Higginson recognized the value of resuming his record:

I need a book in which to write not what I wish to do, but what I am led to do.

What afterward becomes of these thoughts is a secondary thing. I can readily understand the materialistic doctrine of thought as a kind of perspiration of the brain, when I find myself 'proaching it as I do at times. . . .

I am weary of these lives that end early & leave only blossoms, not fruit, for a remembrance. Unless it is worthwhile, & I have one stay long enough on Earth & produce something, it is not worth while to be remembered at all. (3/6/49)

This entry suggests that, like many of the Transcendentalists, Higginson was torn between the desire to do something meaningful and the refusal to do anything that did not fit with his spiritual perceptions of value. Bronson Alcott wrote many similar complaints in his journals,[26] and Ralph Waldo Emerson wrote in "The Transcendentalist" (1842), "Unless the action is necessary, unless it is adequate, I do not wish to perform it. . . . I can sit in a corner and perish . . . but I will not move until I have the highest command.

Higginson's diary of this period includes a number of undated comments on spiritual concerns, making this journal seem more like Emerson's than other parts of Higginson's record; however, Higginson was not so much a disciple of Emerson as of William Henry Channing. Emerson in his "Ode" to Channing declined to leave his study for political action but accepted the idea that each should go to "his chosen work." Channing's work was to seek the changes that would for a time "rend the northland from the south." Higginson in this period became very active in the abolitionist movement.

Higginson felt that there was an "unavoidable consciousness in a man of something greater than the body's senses" (3/6/49). His problem was to transcend sensory information and find his proper action by looking at the spiritual reality directly. Searching for things of the spirit he became interested in spiritualism, and one of the most interesting sections of the journals involves his attempt to make a "scientific" study of psychic phenomena such as spirit rappings, the communications of spirits to mediums by mean of knocks on a table or other sounds. Higginson was so impressed that he wished to "lose no time in transcribing for my notes an account of the remarkable results of my 4th experiment of this kind day before." He had watched as a woman who "wished to converse with her [deceased] mother" enlisted the aid of a medium. Though the "raps were quite faint," Higginson watched as the raps spelled out, "be calm my child. . . . your mother watches over you." Higginson claimed that he was convinced because the spirit raps then answered questions to which the medium could not have known the answer (4/29/52).

Probably the most important of Higginson's journals are those written during his service in the Civil War. This journal section began with an entry for November 11, 1862, written on board the steamer *Cosmopolitan* off the coast of Cape Hatteras. Higginson was traveling to the Sea Islands of South Carolina to command a regiment of black infantry, and he later adapted part of this journal in *Army Life in a Black Regiment*. Part of this book, which he subtitled a "Camp Diary," was only slightly changed from the original entries in his journal; part is a separate account.

Higginson looked forward to his new post for a number of reasons. His actions would allow him to work actively to support the Union cause and demonstrate the ability of the blacks he sought to aid. However, another reason, expressed early in this section of the journals, was the romantic attraction of the new, the unexpected. At thirty-nine he saw it as a chance to prove that his life was not over, his fate decided. In the following excerpt his rejection of his mother's position suggests the youthful exuberance of his early journals when, just after graduating from college, he declared his new sense of maturity and his independence from maternal domination:

As I approach the mysterious land I am more and more impressed with my good fortune in having this novel and uncertain career open before me when I thought everything was definitely arranged. My dear mother was wrong in regretting that I exchanged the certain for the uncertain. Everything I hear of this new opportunity the more attractive it becomes. (11/23/62)

This romantic attitude is evident in much of Higginson's descriptions during his stay in South Carolina. Although this portion of the journals was written at about the same time and place as that of Charlotte Forten, the attitudes toward his experiences that Higginson expressed in his record were very different from those Forten wrote in hers. To Higginson, even in the decay of an abandoned plantation with its "broken windows" and "all manner of wrecks & refuse " the South seemed to have a relaxed, romantic beauty suited to such poetic descriptions. Higginson spent as much or more time in his attempts to "describe the picturesque . . . life" around him as he did in describing activities related to the war (4/17/63).

However, Higginson was repeatedly reminded of reality, vitality, and activity by his "regiment of freed slaves," before whose very existence "the whole Southern coast . . . trembles." He came to realize that the slaves had learned to give the impression of "hopeless, impenetrable stupidity," but that it was really a "mask" put on to conceal their "wealth of mother wit" (11/27/62). In scene after scene Higginson put the lie to the "absurd . . . impression about these Southern blacks growing out of a state of slavery, that they are sluggish or inefficient in labor" or intelligence (12/1/62). They work harder than whites and show a fine understanding of human character.

Higginson sought to capture the real language of the camp as a way of preserving its characters. Even by the campfire he tried to write down everything. One particularly moving scene is his description of a ceremony on New Year's day during which the Emancipation Proclamation was read. The blacks broke out spontaneously in singing "My Country, 'Tis of Thee," an experience "so electric; it made all other words cheap; it seemed the choked voice of a race at last unloosed." So powerful was the effect that it inspired its hearers, black and white, to identify themselves with this expression of freedom by joining together in song (1/1/63).

The effect Higginson described here seems related to that which he expressed when, after reviewing his black troops, he had to remind himself that he was not black (11/27/62). When he claimed "a constitutional affinity for undeveloped races," he was endorsing the blacks' potential for development. His label "undeveloped races" was not based on skin color (he included the Irish as an undeveloped race), or association with the idea of the noble savage (he rejected what he called "Thoreau's anti-civilization hobby"). Neither did it seem a paternalism. When so-called "philanthropists" would arrive in the Sea Islands expecting "to be impressed with the degradation and stupidity of these people," Higginson would tell them that he had "not a stupid man in the regiment" (11/21/63).

In describing his soldiers' reaction to battle Higginson stressed their bravery and stoicism: "You who have read this journal will acquit me, in previous sheets, of any carelessness or sweeping boasts of this regiment: but I will now speak freely & say that if I could have one half the time for drill that many regiments now in the service have had, there is not one which I would be afraid to drill." In a section not included in *Army Life* Higginson recorded his claim that, while he knew that it was not easy to win battles, he believed that "if they can be won at all, these are the troops with which to win them" (1/19/63).

Unused to warfare, Higginson found it difficult "to begin journalizing again after the stirring life" of the battlefield, and when he did so, he found it necessary to explain how different the experience was from his expectations:

It was easy to see how little it costs to be courageous in battle. There are a thousand things that require more daring; the reason being that the danger does not come home so vividly to the senses in battle; there is the noise & the smoke & then besides no matter how loud the bullets may whiz, so long as you are not hit, they don't mean you & after they do mean you, it's too late to be frightened. To a person afraid of lightening for instance, a severe storm is more terrifying than a battle, because you sit *silent* waiting for the flash & wondering if the next will strike you—& you have not the excitement of flashing back again. (2/4/63)

There is very little in the small-pages diary book record of the war period to match that in the journals. Even after he ended the simultaneous journal and began to use a book with larger pages, Higginson's diary did not improve. It includes some personal revelations and descriptive passages, but generally this diary consists of short notes. Among the few important entries in the diary are a pair about Emily Dickinson; however, these seem woefully inadequate. In the first, written about a trip to Amherst in 1870, Higginson recorded that his visit "was a remarkable experience quite excelling . . . my expectations," and that Amherst was "a pleasant country town" (8/16/70). His entry describing Dickinson's funeral is markedly fuller than most of those in the diary, but even this entry, treating the passing of someone in whom he detected special merit, is far too brief to be adequate:

To Amherst to the funeral of that rare and strange creature Emily Dickinson. The country exquisite, day perfect & an atmosphere of its own, fine and strange about the whole home & grounds—a more saintly and elevated "House of Usher." The grass of the lawn full of buttercups, violets & wild geraniums; in house a handful of peonies & another of lilies of the valley on piano. E.D.'s face a wondrous restoration of youth—she is 54 & looked 30, not a gray hair or wrinkle, & a perfect peace on the beautiful brow. There was a little bunch of violets at the neck & one pink cypripedium; the sister Vinnie put in two heliotropes by her hand . . . I read a poem by Emily Bronte. How large a portion of the people who have most interested me have passed away. (5/17/86)

Higginson's diary continued until the year of his death, 1911, but it never attained the quality of the earlier journals.

John Burroughs (1837–1921)

Burroughs's diary had its origin in a series of notebooks that he began to keep in 1854 when he was only seventeen; and, as he told Clara Barrus, who would later edit his *Journals,* "Here is where I practiced when I was learning my trade." The statement supports Barrus's claim that "much in the journal is experimental" and that, while Burrough's entries may contain "passages as beautiful as any in his published work," they are mostly "undressed thoughts."[27]

These "undressed thoughts" of the notebooks are often as fully developed as those one would expect to find in even the most carefully written diaries. The following early, undated excerpt suggests that the best poet is he whose work most fully expresses the Transcendentalists' contention that the physical world is but a symbol of a spiritual reality: "Poetry is spiritual facts represented by natural symbols; hence the most poetic writer, as well as the most pleasing and instructive, is he who conveys his ideas in illustrations drawn from natural objects, who makes the world of matter mirror forth the world of mind" (4–5). This use of "natural objects" to mirror the "world of the mind" is a common feature of most journals of the Transcendentalists, and certainly Burroughs's diary belongs in this category.

Some of Burroughs' notebook entries seem to echo passages from Thoreau in style as well as in content. Part of the similarity can be attributed to the two men's shared interest in nature. Especially after Burroughs's notebook became a full and regular diary, he used it to capture his reaction to nature. Like Thoreau, he found beauty everywhere. He delighted not just in "the strawberry days" with their "daisies and buttercups, the song of the birds, their first madness and lovemaking over," (77) but also "how beautifully . . . [a queen bee's] body tapers" (76) or the way "the webs of little spiders in the road" when "saturated with minute drops of moisture exhibit prismatic tints" and become "fairy napkins" (332). There frequently is something sensual in Burroughs's description of natural scenes. It is not just in his inclusion of sex as a valid part of nature, but also a passion in his own relation to it. Burroughs believed that one could not write well about nature unless one could write "with feeling, with real love" (209). Indeed, for Burroughs "the great poet and the great naturalist" were one, and one cannot read his diaries without recognizing that his writing sprang from a genuine reverence for all things natural (70).

If Burroughs in his diary seems to have had much in common with Thoreau, one of their strongest similarities is their common debt to Emerson. In an entry written shortly after Emerson's death Burroughs, reproaching himself for not going to the funeral, explained, "I should have been there. Emerson was my spiritual father in the strictest sense. It seems I owe nearly all or whatever I am to him" (87–88). This passage comes into better focus when paired with one from an entry written after the death of his biological father:

Father knew me not. All my aspirations in life were a sealed book to him, as much as his particular religious experiences were to me. Yet I reckon it was the same heaven working in us both. The delight he had in his Bible, in his hymn-book, in his Church, in his creed, I have in literature, in the poets, in Nature. His was related in his thought to his soul's salvation hereafter, mine to my soul's salvation here. (106)

The spiritual distance between father and son was emphasized later in the same entry, when Burroughs explained that his father denied him not only the sympathy, but also the financial assistance that had been granted all of Burroughs's siblings. Burroughs's claim that he had been "better unhelped as it proved. . . . and perhaps I loved him the better for denying me," is difficult to fully accept. A reader is likely to be particularly suspicious after reading Burroughs's protest, "I never laid up anything against him, not even the fact that once, when I was away at school and got short of funds, and wanted five dollars to help me out he would not send it" (108). The recollection of this incident after almost thirty years suggests its traumatic nature. The tension between father and son about education helps to account for the initiation of the first notebooks at the time when Burroughs left for school.[28]

Burroughs made friendships with a number of the Transcendentalists, and his encounters with them make for some of the most interesting entries. In the following anecdote from his notebooks Burroughs tells of Walt Whitman's reaction to a statement attributed to Emerson that he [Emerson] was not yet "satisfied" with Whitman's books, for

he expected him "to make—the songs of the Nation—but he seems—
to be contented to—make the inventories":

Walt laughed and said it tickled him much. It was capital. But it did not
disturb him at all. "I know what I am about better than Emerson does. Yet I
love to hear what the gods have to say." And continuing, he said: "I see how
I might easily have wandered into other and easier paths than I did—paths
that would have paid better, and gained me popularity; and I wonder how my
feet were guided as they were. Indeed I am more than satisfied with myself
for having the courage to do what I have." (56)

The journals have numerous invaluable personal glimpses of Whitman and other famous men with whom Burroughs was acquainted.
Some such entries found their way into Burroughs's published writings, for, like Emerson and Thoreau, Burroughs recognized the potential of journal material. He also made use of the diaries of others in his
writings. The most extensive of these is "Emerson and His Journals,"
a piece over twenty thousand words long which was published as part
of Burroughs's book, *The Last Harvest*.

Burroughs's journals trace his growing success. His books brought
him fame beyond his expectations. He became friends not only with
the Transcendentalists but with men of wealth and power such as Theodore Roosevelt, Thomas Edison, and Henry Ford. Burroughs, who had
long been concerned about his limited education, was able to record
his receipt of honorary degrees and other awards.

However, Burroughs never seems to have been fully satisfied or secure. Perhaps this is one reason why death plays such a major role in
many of the journal's entries. A long description of his mother's death
and his own reaction to it is particularly moving—and such entries
became more frequent as Burroughs aged and more of his acquaintances
died.[29] He comments on the deaths of Emerson, Whitman, Muir, Roosevelt, Howells, and other notable figures with whom he was personally acquainted, and his journal reveals the growing sorrow of a man
who "outlives his generation and feels alone in the world. . . . [he]
has no alternative but to live in the past . . . with the dead, and they
pull him down" (330). One of the most touching entries deals with
the death of his wife. Her memory does not provoke unrestrained sorrow; indeed, he calls her "a discord in my life," but his assessment
makes the passage the more real, the more effective:

Very lonely. Oh the falling leaves! They move me. Her house is like a tomb. Felt her loss afresh when I went over to the kitchen door and found the leaves clustered there as if waiting for something. They were waiting for her broom. For over forty years it had not failed them, and now they lay there, dulled and discouraged. Oh, the unswept stones and entry-way—what a tale they tell!

I never could have believed I should miss her so much. Yet I do not want her back—but if only I could know she was well and happy somewhere in the land of the living!

Over forty years we two sat here and saw our days go by; saw the leaves come and go and the seasons change. Now they come and go no more—the dust in her house, the leaves at her door, are undisturbed. (312)

The approach of Burroughs's own aging and death is also a concern in the later years of the journals. He had long before declared his inability to accept the traditional faith that his parents had found so comforting, but unlike most Transcendentalists, Burroughs was unable to find a sufficient alternative belief. Whitman had declared his conviction that the dead were absorbed in the development of new life, writing in *Leaves of Grass* that "the smallest sprout shows that there is no death, / and if ever there was it led forward to life." However, Burroughs did not find Whitman's solution fully satisfying. While he believed that "nothing can be lost" because the elements of the body and the forces of the mind were eternal, he feared that "the consciousness, the *me*," ended with death (249). Even the attempt to face death happily seemed misplaced. In an entry written less than two years before his death Burroughs wrote, "If we were under judicial sentence to be shot or electrocuted at no distant day, would not the thought of it harass us day and night? But we go about with Nature's death-sentence upon us, even in old age, when we know the day is near, as cheerful and contented as ever we did" (325). His final position on death seems reminiscent of William Cullen Bryant's argument in "Thanatopsis." Bryant had written that, although in death one may lose his "individual being . . . to mix forever with the elements, / To be a brother to the insensible rock," nature taught that one may learn to approach death with trust by living life. To the end Burroughs strove for a full life. His last entry, written while recovering from an illness, includes the words, "life seems worth living again" (339).

Chapter Nine
Conclusion: Looking Forward

The diary did not cease to be either a common or an important form with the coming of the twentieth century. Blank diary books sell well in the bookstores, and the same type of tensions and dislocations that produced the diaries in this volume continue to prompt new works. However, because most diaries are written as private or semiprivate documents, such records do not usually become available to the public until after, often long after, the diarist has died. Even some of the better diaries of the late nineteenth century may not be made public for many years. Tragedy brought us the diaries of Anne Frank and Sylvia Plath, but there are certainly numerous excellent twentieth century diaries that will be published, and many of these will be by American diarists.

Just as in this volume we were able to examine some of the best diaries of the Civil War, so we should soon find comparable records by both soldiers and civilians that deal with World War II, the Korean War, and even the Vietnam War. Perhaps some time in the future we may even read diaries of the first people to settle beyond the limits of earth, just as we can now read those of pioneers in the American West.

While some excellent twentieth-century diaries such as that of Arthur Crew Inman have been published, it will be many years before a volume similar to this could be written about twentieth-century diarists with any hope of being reasonably complete. Nevertheless, it is not too early to see some signs of the developments that are taking place in the diary form.

Some changes in diaries may be mostly cosmetic. Certainly, many diaries have been composed on typewriters and on tape recorders, and I don't doubt that a number are already being saved on word-processor floppy disks. But in terms of the diary as a literary form, one should be more concerned with other influences of the modern world. Some ideas about what to expect can be gained by looking at other literary forms. Just as so many twentieth-century poems and novels have expressed their authors' concerns about the sterility of modern society, racial prejudice, women's rights, and fears of nuclear war, so we may expect such concerns to figure prominently in the diaries of this period.

The division between public and private genres has never been as great as most people have believed, and modern diarists are especially likely to be concerned about revelations in a diary, but more writers in other genres have become conscious of similar problems. In *The Novel of the Future* Anaïs Nin, famous both as a diarist and a fiction writer, admitted that both her "diary and fiction tended toward the same goal: intimacy with people, with experience, with life itself." She claimed that while her diary with its "spontaneous writing in the present came closer to the truth" than did her stories because as the teller changed so did "the versions of the past," there was a "taboo on certain revelations" in the diary that resulted in a "personal censorship" that was not present in fiction writing.[1] In *The Forms of Autobiography* William C. Spengemann approached this same situation from a different direction, arguing persuasively that even when a fiction writer abandons "all reference to the biographical event" and adopts "totally fictive materials," the autobiographical impulse may survive in an effort "to discover, through a fictive action, some ground upon which conflicting aspects of the writer's own nature might be reconciled."[2]

However, even as the diary form becomes more widely accepted and studied as a literary work, it will take many years before it is understood the way genres more traditionally considered "literary" are understood. It will, therefore, also be a long time in the future before a large number of diarists become sufficiently knowledgeable about the nature of the form that they and their critics express concern about the "death of the diary." If recent scholarly attention is any indication, serious attention to the diary as an art form will continue to grow for many years.

Notes and References

Chapter One

    1. F. O. Matthiessen, *American Renaissance* (New York, 1941), vii.
    2. Thomas Wentworth Higginson, *Letters and Journals of Thomas Wentworth Higginson 1846–1906,* ed. Mary Thacher Higginson (Boston, 1921), 348.

Chapter Two

    1. Edwin Bryant, *What I Saw in California* . . . (New York, 1848), 17. Hereafter references to this edition are cited by page number in parentheses in the text.
    2. Emigrating to California, the members of the Donner party were trapped by a snowstorm in a mountain pass during the winter of 1846–47, and some had to resort to cannibalism to survive (256–60).
    3. Rev. Walter Colton, *Three Years in California* (New York, 1850), (112–13). Hereafter references to this edition are cited by page number in parentheses in the text.
    4. There are numerous other diaries of the California gold rush. Many of these have been highly revised from the original versions, and some are autobiographies in diary form or fictional creations.
    5. Daniel B. Woods, *Sixteen Months at the Gold Diggings* (New York, 1851), vii. Hereafter references to this edition are cited by page number in parentheses in the text.
    6. Carpenter's initial phrase "Ho—for California" became part of the title for the volume in which it has been published, *Ho for California! Women's Overland Diaries from the Huntington Library,* ed. Sandra L. Myres (San Marino, 1980), 93. Hereafter references to this edition are cited by page number in parentheses in the text. This volume includes four other diaries; all are interesting but none is of the quality of Carpenter's.

Chapter Three

    1. John Beatty, *Memoirs of a Volunteer,* ed. Harvey S. Ford (New York, 1946), 18. Hereafter references to this edition are cited by page number in parentheses in the text.
    2. Benjamin T. Smith, *Private Smith's Journal,* ed. Clyde C. Walton (Chicago, 1963), 214–15. Hereafter references to this edition are cited by page number in parentheses in the text.

3. John L. Ransom, *Andersonville Diary* (Philadelphia, 1881). References to this edition are cited by page number in parentheses in the text.

4. Charles Herbert, diarist of *A Relic of the Revolution,* ed. Rev. R. Livesey (Boston, 1844). This diary is discussed at length in Steven E. Kagle, *American Diary Literature 1607–1800* (Boston, 1979), 114–21.

5. Salmon P. Chase, *Inside Lincoln's Cabinet: The Civil War Diaries of Salmon P. Chase,* ed. David Donald (New York, 1954), 118–19. Chase and Welles were only two of a number of members of the government who kept diaries during the Civil War.

6. Gideon Welles, *The Diary of Gideon Welles,* ed. Howard K. Beal (New York, 1960), 104–5. Hereafter all references to this edition are cited by volume and page number in parentheses in the text. This version is far better for diary study than the first published version (1911), which was heavily revised, mostly by Welles himself, and which does not distinguish between true diary material and material written long after the original entries.

Chapter Four

1. Adam Gurowski, *Diary 1862–1866,* 3 vols. (Washington, 1866).

2. Judith McGuire, *Diary of a Southern Refugee During the War* (New York, 1867), 5. Hereafter references to this edition are cited in parentheses in the text.

3. Sarah Morgan Dawson, *A Confederate Girl's Diary,* ed. James I. Robertson Jr. (Bloomington, Ind., 1960), xxvii-xxxi. Hereafter references to this edition are cited in parentheses in the text.

4. Two months after the start of the diary her home town of Baton Rouge, Louisiana, was taken by the Union army.

5. Sarah Katherine Stone Holmes, *Brokenburn,* ed. John Q. Anderson (Baton Rouge, 1955), 3. Hereafter references to this edition are cited in parentheses in the text.

6. Holmes began her diary in May, 1861, when her eldest brother left for the Civil War; and, although its last entry is dated September, 1862, she made only a few entries after the war's end.

7. Eliza Frances Andrews, *The Wartime Diary of a Georgia Girl 1864–1865,* ed. Spencer Bidwell King, Jr. (Macon, 1960), xiii-xvii. Hereafter references to this edition are cited in parentheses in the text.

8. (124–26, 139–43). This practical joking seems reminiscent of that in Sally Wister's diary kept during the Revolutionary War. See: Kagle, *American Diary Literature,* 86–92.

9. In a note added during the editing of the diary Andrews admitted that some of her harsh words about some Union soldiers were unfounded and stemmed rather from the hatred "that rankled in every Southern breast and converted each individual Yankee into a vicarious black sheep" (261–62, 266).

10. Mary Boykin Chesnut, *The Private Mary Chesnut,* ed. C. Vann

Woodward and Elisabeth Muhlenfeld (New York, 1984)—the original diary; hereafter references to it are cited in parentheses in the text by page number preceded by the letter *P.* Mary Boykin Chesnut, *Mary Chesnut's Civil War,* ed. C. Vann Woodward (New Haven, 1981), xv–xxxiv—the revised version; hereafter references to it are cited in parentheses in the text by page number preceded by the letter *M.*

11. Chesnut's husband resigned his Senate seat to join the secessionist movement.

12. Charles Sumner (1811–1874), senator from Massachusetts and one of the most fervent abolitionists.

13. Ray Allen Billington, "Introduction," in Charlotte L. Forten, *The Journal of Charlotte L. Forten, A Free Negro in the Slave Era,* ed. Ray Allen Billington (New York, 1981), 7. Hereafter references are to this edition and are cited in parentheses in the text.

14. Diana M. Mulock Craik's *Life for a Life* (London, 1859). See: Charlotte L. Forten, *Journal,* 131, 261n.

15. See Kagle, *American Diary Literature 1607–1800,* 67–71.

16. Forten read Kemble's diary sometime after it was published in 1863. She noted in her own diary that Kemble's was "painfully interesting, and bears the impress of truth on every line. It fills one with admiration for the noble woman whose true humanity shrank with the utmost loathing from the terrible system whose details she saw every day" (221). Another diary describing slavery in the Sea Islands of South Carolina is that of Thomas B. Chaplin published as part of Theodore Rosengarten's *Tombee* (New York, 1986).

17. This was the battle in which Colonel Robert Gould Shaw (celebrated in Robert Lowell's poem, "For the Union Dead") was killed. Forten has a number of entries dealing with Shaw.

18. Forten made some later diary entries over twenty years later but these are only fragments (39).

Chapter Five

1. Mollie Dorsey Sanford, *Mollie: The Journal of Mollie Dorsey Sanford in Nebraska and Colorado Territories 1857–1866,* ed. Donald F. Danker (Lincoln, 1959), 3. Hereafter references to this edition appear in parentheses in the text.

2. Dorsey might have felt even more strongly about the move; however, she was resigned to it as necessary because of her father's financial "reverses" which made it difficult for him to support a family of eight. The prospect of cheap land was a strong encouragement for emigration to the recently opened territory.

3. Alice James, *Diary* (Cambridge, 1894); Alice James, "Her Journal," in Anna Robeson Burr, *Alice James: Her Brothers—Her Journal* (New York,

1934); Alice James, *The Diary of Alice James,* ed. Leon Edel (New York, 1964). All references to James's diary appear in parentheses in the text and refer to the Edel edition.

4. Alice James certainly had some share of the talent possessed by her famous brothers Henry and William. Indeed she claimed that Henry James had "embedded in his pages many pearls fallen from my lips" and that he had stolen them "in the most unblushing way, saying, simply, that he knew they had been said by the family, so that it did not matter" (212).

5. Here James is referring to the assertion by her companion Kathleen Loring: "What an awful pity it is that you can't say *damn.*" James added, "I agreed with her from my heart. It is an immense loss to have all robust and sustaining expletives refined away from one" (66).

Chapter Six

1. Richard Henry Dana Jr., *The Journal of Richard Henry Dana Jr.,* ed. Robert F. Lucid (Cambridge: Harvard University Press, 1968), 1:28. Hereafter references to this edition are cited by volume and page number in the text.

2. One brief and sketchy set of dated journal entries exists. (See "Journal of a Voyage from Boston to the Coast of California, by Richard Henry Dana," ed. James Allison, *American Neptune* 12 (1952):177–85. However, Robert F. Metzdorf in "The Publishing History of *Two Years Before the Mast,*" *Harvard Library Bulletin* 7 (1953):312–13 notes that a more complete journal existed, but that it was lost because of the carelessness of Dana's cousin. If so, along with the journals of Alcott's Fruitlands period, these are among the most important missing American diaries (See: Richard Henry Dana, Jr., *Journals,* 1:28).

3. 1:12, 19, 25. Also see: Kagle, *American Diary Literature 1607– 1800, 121–27.*

4. In his "Introduction" Robert F. Lucid notes: "The format of Dana's *Journal,* to a fanciful imagination, could stand as the symbol of the events which the *Journal* traces. The record begins with elaborate formality: besides the eighty-page autobiographical sketch, there is a long family history. Day-by-day entries are made in detail, neatly and promptly. Nearly twenty years later, as the *Journal* draws to a close, the entries are ragged; there are yawning gaps between them and even the handwriting has become tremulous, sometimes all but indecipherable" (1:xxx).

5. *Hawthorne's Lost Notebook, 1835–1841* contains some additional material as well as a correct version of some entries in the *American Notebooks* taken from an imperfect copy made by Sophia Hawthorne. It seems likely that Hawthorne kept other diary books of which no record exists. A volume entitled *Hawthorne's First Diary,* published in 1897, is considered a forgery. See

Simpson's note (*A*, 677). This reference and all subsequent references to Hawthorne's diaries refer to the following editions, and appear in parentheses in the text preceded by a letter to indicate the volume cited: *A* for *American Notebooks*, ed. Claude M. Simpson (Columbus, 1972); *E* for *English Notebooks*, ed. Randall Stewart (New York, 1962); *F* for *French and Italian Notebooks*, ed. Thomas Woodson (Columbus, 1980); and *L* for *Hawthorne's Lost Notebook*, ed. Barbara S. Mouffe (University Park, 1978).

6. Horatio Bridge, *Journal of an African Cruiser*, ed. Nathaniel Hawthorne (New York, 1853).

7. There are two sections of material similar to that of this life diary. One was written in 1841 during part of Hawthorne's residence at Brook Farm (an experience which was a major inspiration for *The Blithedale Romance*) and the other kept intermittently in 1847–1851, focusing on his children (part of the latter section is entitled "Twenty Days with Julian & Little Bunny").

8. The last of these examples contains the basic plot of *The Scarlet Letter.*

9. Nathaniel Hawthorne, *Blithedale Romance* (Columbus, 1964), 229–37.

10. Nathaniel Hawthorne, "Ethan Brand" in *Snow Image*, ed. William Charvat et al. (Columbus, 1974), 84.

11. Nathaniel Hawthorne, *Our Old Home*, ed. William Charvat et al. (Columbus, 1970), 4–5.

12. (*E*, 88–89). Hawthorne used this material in passages of *Our Old Home* and *The Ancestral Footstep*. *The Ancestral Footstep* was written in diary form with dated entries, and Hawthorne wrote another work, "Fragments from the Journal of a Solitary Man," in diary form but without dated entries.

13. (*E*, 126). This material appears in *Our Old Home* and "Grimshawe." "Grimshaw" is the title Hawthorne's editors have given to one of the manuscript fragments which Julian Hawthorne used to construct *Dr. Grimshaw's Secret* after his father's death.

14. Henry Arthur Bright. *Happy Country This America: The Travel Diaries of Henry Arthur Bright*, ed. Anne Ehrenpreis (Columbus, 1978).

15. In *Our Old Home* Hawthorne wrote: "These and other sketches, with which in a somewhat rougher form . . . my Journal was copiously filled, were intended for the side scenes, and backgrounds, and exterior adornments of a work of fiction" (3–4).

16. Frederick Crews discussed Hawthorne's anti-Semitism as it appeared in *The Marble Faun*, declaring that "such prose . . . reminds us more of *Mein Kampf* than of the theological works that are usually adduced to explain Hawthorne's ideas" *Sins of the Fathers* (New York, 1966), 222. However, there has been a surprising lack of attention to such material in Hawthorne's notebooks. The passages containing his anti-Semitic remarks are omitted from anthologies and even from the various abbreviated editions of the notebooks. Equally significant is the fact that there is almost no commentary on the anti-Semitic passages in the notebooks in the mass of criticism on Hawthorne. It is ne-

glected in the biographies, and even Randall Stewart in his edition of the *English Notebooks* failed to make any comment on it in his notes. Two exceptions are Louis Harap's *The Image of the Jew in American Literature* (Philadelphia, 1974), 108–10, and M. Herschel Levine's "Oedipal Views of the Jew in American Literature," *Journal of Psychology and Judaism* 3 (1978):102–8.

17. Nathaniel Hawthorne, *The Marble Faun,* ed. William Charvat et al. (Columbus, 1968), 48.

18. The significance of Hawthorne's "dark and fair ladies" has received treatment in Philip Rahv, "Dark Lady of Salem," *Partisan Review* 7 (1941):362–81, and is a major concern in Philip Young's *Hawthorne's Secret: an Un-told Tale* (Boston, 1984).

19. (337) See also Bruno Bettleheim's *Uses of Enchantment.*

20. Nathaniel Hawthorne, "Artist of the Beautiful" in *Mosses from an Old Manse,* ed. William Charvat et al. (Columbus, 1974), 475.

21. Dallas kept a diary during some if not all of the eighteen years between the two published diplomatic diaries and probably before and after the published portions. However, with the exception of a photostat of the diary for the period 12/48–3/49 in the collection of the Pennsylvania Historical Society, whatever manuscripts survive are in private or semiprivate collections. All references to the published diaries are from: George Mifflin Dallas, *Diary of George Mifflin Dallas,* ed. Susan Dallas (Philadelphia, 1892) and are cited by page number in parentheses in the text; references to manuscript materials are in parentheses by entry date.

22. This was not Dallas's first trip to London. He had gone there in 1813 when he was secretary to Albert Gallatin. His experiences on this earlier trip connect him with two other important American diarists, James Gallatin and John Quincy Adams. See Kagle, *Early Nineteenth-Century American Diary Literature* (Boston, 1986), 65–68, 81–102.

23. A further, and perhaps closer, comparison could be made with the attitudes expressed by John Adams in the diplomatic portions of his diary. John Adams shared some of Dallas's uncertainties about externals, but his conviction of personal destiny overrode them. I am indebted in this line of investigation to the suggestions of Peter Parker of the Pennsylvania Historical Society. See also: E. Digby Baltzell, *Puritan Boston and Quaker Philadelphia* (New York, 1979); Peter Shaw, *The Character of John Adams* (Chapel Hill, 1976); and Kagle, *American Diary Literature, 1607–1800,* 170–82.

24. This brief manuscript diary is in the collection of the Pennsylvania Historical Society.

25. It was during Buchanan's administration that Moran met Hawthorne.

26. Benjamin Moran, *The Footpath and Highway or Wanderings of an American in Great Britain in 1851 & 1852* (Phialdelphia, 1853).

27. Benjamin Moran, *The Journal of Benjamin Moran 1857–1865,* ed. Sarah Agnes Wallace and Frances Elma Gillespie (Chicago, 1949). Hereafter

references to this edition are cited by volume and page number in parentheses in the text. The extant manuscript of Moran's diary is in the Library of Congress; references to manuscript entries are cited by entry date in parentheses in the text.

28. One indication of the source of Moran's reaction here is the fact that the young doctor he condemned for "Philadelphia snobbism," though married to a woman from Philadelphia, was from South Carolina, but George Mifflin Dallas was from Philadelphia. Moran himself was raised near Philadelphia.

29. Though the editors of the diary wrote that Moran made a "hasty marriage" to "a mill girl," Moran described his wife as "well educated" (1:viii, 168).

30. The last mention of Miss Bird in the diary is in 1860, but the editors note that "a Miss Bird, presumably Alice attended Moran's funeral in 1886" (1:55n).

31. Charles Francis Adams, *Diary of Charles Francis Adams,* entry for 5/15/61. Hereafter all references to Adams's diary are by entry date and appear in parentheses in the text. See chapter 7, note 1.

32. When, during the Civil War, Moran heard that Dallas had declared himself "a Union man & wants to get into Congress," he recalled how Dallas had helped the rebels to buy arms, and called this political declaration "a demagogue's attempt to switch to the winning side" (2:837). Yet, when in 1865 Moran heard of Dallas's death, he wrote, "Badly as he behaved to me, he was at heart a gentleman. His course was prompted by his family" (2:1367).

33. Moran's error in originally writing St. James's instead of Lisbon may have been only the result of habit after his long service there, but it may be a Freudian slip indicating his aspirations.

Chapter Seven

1. Adams often prepared an "index" of his diary, a summary of entries in dated diary form. Even the "Journal of Vacation" was not a true diary but was written the following spring from notes and memory. A regular diary kept at the time was lost. See: Charles Francis Adams, *Diary of Charles Francis Adams,* ed L. H. Butterfield et al. (Cambridge, 1964–), 1:xxxiv-xxxvi, 1–9, 96–97. Subsequent references to the introduction and notes of this edition appear by volume and page number in parentheses in the text. Although the first two volumes of this diary were published in 1964, as of this writing the last to appear were volumes seven and eight in 1986. The balance of the diary, though unpublished, is available in microfilm form at many research libraries as part of the *Adams Papers.* Since the last published volume ends with entries written in 1840, and since Adams kept his diary until 1880, the bulk of the work including that covering his political career is not available in print. Therefore, all references to it are cited by entry date in parentheses in the text.

2. No candidate received a majority of electoral votes; therefore, the election was decided by a vote in the House of Representatives.

3. (11/16–17/34) Charles had expected to help his parents with financial difficulties, debts his father had incurred from "an unprofitable business venture" with Charles's brother John Adams II. Martin Duberman, *Charles Francis Adams* (Stanford, 1968), 52.

4. One of the more important entries is one in which John Quincy Adams influenced his son to accept the nomination. This effort came too late for nomination in 1839, but may have convinced Charles to accept the nomination in 1840 (11/2/39).

5. Duberman, *Adams,* 71.

6. In 1862 Major General Benjamin F. Butler, commander of the Union forces occupying New Orleans, had responded to insults to Union troops by some of the city's women by issuing a proclamation that in the future any women committing such acts should be assumed to be prostitutes and treated as such.

7. Sidney George Fisher, *A Philadelphia Perspective; the Diary of Sidney George Fisher Covering the Years 1834–1871,* ed. Nicholas B. Wainwright (Philadelphia, 1967), 2–7. Hereafter references to this edition are cited in parentheses in the text.

8. Of course Fisher's prophetic power seems less to be trusted when one notes other entries such as that in which he wrote in September, 1856, arguing that the Southern threat to dissolve the Union if the Republican candidate (in this case Frémont) was elected president was not serious and that "unless thro some sudden excitement & madness, they will never dissolve the Union" (260).

9. The intensity of Fisher's concern about these matters is evident from the close repetition of phrasing of the same idea in entries written 12/22/36 and 2/9/37 (16, 21).

10. Fisher abandoned his regular diary in September, 1870, but kept up some entries in a memorandum book until July 22, 1871 three days before his death.

11. Strong's diary was kept for a longer period of time. He began his diary when he was just fifteen and continued it almost until his death nearly fifty years later.

12. George Templeton Strong, *The Diary of George Templeton Strong,* ed. Allan Nevins and Milton Halsey Thomas (New York, 1952), 2:24. Hereafter references to this edition are cited by volume and page number in parentheses in the text.

Chapter Eight

1. Transcendentalism and diaries of two important American Transcendentalists, Ralph Waldo Emerson and A. Bronson Alcott, are discussed at

length in another book in this series: Kagle, *Early Nineteenth-Century American Diary Literature,* 103–44.

2. Thoreau's journal was first published in a relatively complete form in Henry David Thoreau, *Journal,* ed. Bradford Torrey, vols. 7–20, *The Writings of Henry David Thoreau* (Boston, 1906). This work has been reprinted in several editions, most recently as *The Journals of Henry David Thoreau,* 2 vols. (New York, 1962). This edition is in the preocess of being superseded by a new Center for Editions of American Authors version prepared under the general editorship of John C. Broderick (Princeton University Press, 1981–). Since at this writing only two volumes have been published and since many readers may first approach this large work through any of a number of abridgments, I have listed references to the journals by entry date. The date for this reference is 3/7/38. All subsequent references are in parentheses in the text.

3. Thoreau takes note of this process in his entry for 2/8/41. Also see: William Ellery Channing II, *Thoreau the Poet Naturalist,* ed. F. B. Sanborn (Boston, 1902), 65–66. This connection is cited in the notes to Bradford Torrey's edition.

4. Paul Elmer More, "Thoreau's Journal" in Paul Elmer More, *Shelburne Essays: Fifth Series* (Boston, 1908). 106–131.

5. Odell Shepard, "Introduction" to Henry David Thoreau, *The Heart of Thoreau's Journals,* ed. Odell Shepard (New York, 1961), viii.

6. Perry Miller, "Introduction" to Henry David Thoreau, *Consciousness in Concord: The Text of Thoreau's Hitherto "Lost Journal" (1840–1841),* ed. Perry Miller (Boston, 1958), 4.

7. Laurence Stapleton's "Introduction" to *H. D. Thoreau: A Writer's Journal* (New York, 1960), ix. Howarth in *The Book of Concord* notes a number of other scholars who have praised the *Journal* as great art.

8. Sharon Cameron, *Writing Nature* (New York, 1985), 3. Cameron also notes that one problem in "regarding the *Journal* as draft material for *Walden* or for Thoreau's other writings" is that it is not "a version of the same enterprise, either inferior or superior to it, but attempts something different" (6).

9. William Howarth, *The Book of Concord* (New York, 1982), 15–25.

10. John C. Broderick, et al., "Historical Introduction" to Henry David Thoreau, *Journal,* 1:593.

11. Henry David Thoreau, *Early Essays and Miscellanies,* ed. Joseph J. Moldenhauer and Edwin Moser (Princeton, 1975), 8.

12. Broderick, "Historical Introduction" to *Journal,* 1:583–84; Stapleton, *H. D. Thoreau: A Writer's Journal,* xxv.

13. See: J. Lyndon Shanley, *The Making of Walden* (Chicago, 1957).

14. Henry David Thoreau, *Walden,* ed. J. Lyndon Shanley (Princeton, 1971), 326; hereafter all references to this edition are cited by page number in the text.

15. Cameron (*Writing Nature*) argues that "because journals, in general,

do not have continuous narratives, and because this [Thoreau's] journal exploits that fact, we have to construct connections between its various subjects" (17).

16. This statement is intended to apply only to a set of passages and not to suggest that *Walden* would so universally be considered better than the *Journal* as a whole.

17. See: Kagle, *American Diary Literature 1607–1800,* 29–46.

18. In 1862 Emily Dickinson wrote Higginson seeking his advice on her poetry, thus starting a long correspondence and leading to his role (with Mabel Loomis Todd) as one of the first editors of Dickinson's writings.

19. See: Forten: 55, 64, 72, 155, 172–75, 189–90, 199–202, 215.

20. Howard Mumford Jones, "Introduction" in Thomas Wentworth Higginson, *Army Life in a Black Regiment* (East Lansing, 1960), vii.

21. Unfortunately most of the published material from Higginson's diary are part of two works of limited use for diary study: Thomas Wentworth Higginson, *Letters and Journals of Thomas Wentworth Higginson 1846–1906,* ed. Mary Thacher Higginson (Boston, 1921), is almost unusable for the study of Higginson's diary because it contains only a tiny fraction of the original manuscript diary, and because it infrequently indicates which of its selections are from letters and which from the diary; Thomas Wentworth Higginson, *Army Life in a Black Regiment* (East Lansing, 1960) is a revised version of the diary. This work only covers the period from the end of November, 1862, to the end of March, 1863, and only a part of that is still in diary entry form. Tilden G. Edelstein, *Strange Enthusiasm: A Life of Thomas Wentworth Higginson,* (New Haven, 1968), includes a good deal of diary material, and thought it was not Edelstein's purpose to structure an examination of the diary, the material he presents does a good job in this regard. Indeed, his selections often imply patterns that Edelstein does not note in his biography. Regrettably, only the last quarter of Edelstein's work covers the last forty-five years of Higginson's life and diary. Most of Higginson's diary survives only in the forty-seven volume manuscript at the Houghton Library, Harvard University (three additional volumes are missing). Therefore, my references to Higginson's diary are listed by entry date in parentheses in the text.

22. Edelstein, *Strange Enthusiasm,* viii. The manuscript of Louisa Higginson's diary is in the collection of the Houghton Library, Harvard University.

23. Edelstein, *Strange Enthusiasm,* 17.

24. In addition to the unusual dislocations, Higginson's father had debts which after his death required the family to sell their home. Ibid., 17, 27.

25. Higginson's struggle to assert his independence, especially from the dominance of his mother is treated in Edelstein, *Strange Enthusiasm,* 33–34.

26. For a considertion of Alcott see Kagle, *Early Nineteenth Century American Diary Literature,* 127–144.

27. Barrus makes a distinction between these early notebooks and the "journals [which] as journals begin abruptly May 13, 1876." Clara Barrus, "Preface" and editorial commentary in John Burroughs, *The Heart of Burroughs's Journals,* ed. Clara Barrus (Boston, 1928), v–vi, xi, 62. All references to Burroughs's journals are to this edition and appear by page number in parentheses in the text. A more complete version of the manuscript is in the John Burroughs Collection, Clifton Waller Barret Library, University of Virginia Library.

28. The importance of his relationship with his parents is further emphasized almost twenty years later when he wrote that he thought most of "the old Home and Father and Mother" (226). A parallel may exist between the origin of this diary and that kept by Michael Wigglesworth two centuries earlier. See Kagle, *American Diary Literature 1607–1800,* 31–38.

29. Some additional journal entries are published in Clara Barrus, *The Life and Letters of John Burroughs,* 2 vols. (Boston, 1925). The entries on his mother's death are in volume 1, 218–20.

Chapter Nine

1. Anaïs Nin, *The Novel of the Future* (New York, 1970), 155.

2. William C. Spengemann, *The Forms of Autobiography* (New Haven, 1980), 132.

Selected Bibliography

PRIMARY SOURCES

1. American Diaries of the Second Half of the Nineteenth Century
Anonymous. *Diary of a Public Man.* Introduction by Carl Sandburg. New Brunswick, Rutgers University Press, 1946. In his introduction Sandburg called this record of the period from 12/28/60 to 3/15/61, "one of the Civil War classics." Unfortunately, its authenticity has always been in doubt.

Adams, Charles Francis. *Diary of Charles Francis Adams.* Edited by L. H. Butterfield, et al. Vol. 1–8. Series I. *The Adams Papers.* Cambridge: Harvard University Press, 1964–1986. These volumes cover the years 1820 to 1840 (the diary continues until 1880) terminating before the most important years of the diary. Fortunately the manuscript of the diary at the Massachusetts Historical Society is available on microfilm.

————. *Diary of Charles Francis Adams. The Adams Papers.* Reels 53–88. Boston: Massachusetts Historical Society, 1954.

Andrews, Eliza Frances. *The Wartime Diary of a Georgia Girl 1864–1865.* Edited by Spencer Bidwell King Jr. Macon: Ardivian Press, 1960.

Beatty, John. *Memoirs of a Volunteer.* Edited by Harvey S. Ford. New York: W. W. Norton, 1946. Originally published under the title *The Citizen Soldier or, Memoirs of a Volunteer.* Cincinnati: Wilstach Baldwin & Co., 1879.

Burroughs, John. *The Heart of Burroughs's Journals.* Edited by Clara Barrus. Boston: Houghton Mifflin, 1928. This abridged version of Burroughs's journal is the most complete yet published.

————. MS journal in the John Burroughs Collection, Clifton Waller Barret Library, University of Virginia Library.

Bryant, Edwin. *What I Saw in California: Being the Journal of a Tour by the Emigrant Route and South Pass of the Rocky Mountains, across the Continent of North America, the Great Basin, and through California in the Years 1846, 1847.* New York: D. Appleton & Co., 1848. Reprint. Minneapolis: Ross & Haines, 1967.

Carpenter, Helen McCowen. *Helen Carpenter, a Trip Across the Plains in an Ox Cart, 1857. Ho for California! Women's Overland Diaries from the Huntington Library.* Edited by Sandra L. Myres, 93–188. San Marino: Huntington Library, 1980.

Chase, Salmon P. *Inside Lincoln's Cabinet: The Civil War Diaries of Salmon P. Chase.* Edited by David Donald. New York: Longmans Green & Co., 1954. Reprint. New York: Kraus Reprint Co., 1970.

Chaplain, Thomas B. See Rosengarten.

Chesnut, Mary Boykin. *The Private Mary Chesnut.* Edited by C. Vann Woodward and Elisabeth Muhlenfeld. New York: Oxford University Press, 1984.

———. *Mary Chesnut's Civil War.* Edited by C. Vann Woodward. New Haven: Yale University Press, 1981.

Colton, Rev. Walter. *Three Years in California.* New York: A. S. Barnes & Co., 1850.

Culley, Margo, ed. *A Day at a Time: The Diary Literature of American Women from 1764 to the Present.* New York: Feminist Press, 1985. A valuable anthology including part of Eliza Frances Andrews's diary.

Dallas, George Mifflin. *Diary of George Mifflin Dallas.* Edited by Susan Dallas. Philadelphia: J. B. Lippincott Co., 1892.

———. *Diary: December 1848–March 1849.* MS. Dallas Papers. Pennsylvania Historical Society, Philadelphia.

Dana, Richard Henry Jr. *The Journal of Richard Henry Dana Jr.* 3 vols. Edited by Robert F. Lucid. Cambridge: Harvard University Press, 1968.

———. "Journal of a Voyage from Boston to the Coast of California, by Richard Henry Dana." Edited by James Allison. *American Neptune* 12 (1952):177–85.

Dawson, Sarah Morgan. *A Confederate Girl's Diary.* Edited by James I. Robertson Jr. Bloomington: Indiana University Press, 1960.

Ely, Dr. Edward. *The Wandering of Edward Ely. A Mid-nineteenth Century Seafarer's Diary.* Edited by Anthony and Allison Sirna. New York: Hastings House, 1954.

Fisher, Sidney George. *A Philadelphia Perspective; the Diary of Sidney George Fisher Covering the Years 1834–1871.* Edited by Nicholas B. Wainwright. Philadelphia: Historical Society of Pennsylvania, 1967.

Forten, Charlotte L. *The Journal of Charlotte L. Forten, A Free Negro in the Slave Era.* Edited and with an Introduction by Ray Allen Billington. New York: W. W. Norton & Co., 1981.

Gurowski, Adam. *Diary 1862–1866.* vol. 1, Boston: Lee & Shepard, 1863. vol. 2, New York: Carleton, 1864. vol. 3, Washington: W. H. & O. H. Morrison, 1866.

Hawthorne, Nathaniel. *American Notebooks.* vol. 8. *Centenary Edition of the Works of Nathaniel Hawthorne.* Edited by Claude M. Simpson. Columbus: Ohio State University Press, 1972.

———. *English Notebooks.* Edited by Randall Stewart. New York: Modern Language Association, 1941. Reprint. New York: Russell & Russell, 1962.

————. *French and Italian Notebooks.* vol. 14 *Centenary Edition of the Works of Nathaniel Hawthorne.* Edited by Thomas Woodson. Columbus: Ohio State University Press, 1980.

————. *Hawthorne's Lost Notebook.* Edited by Barbara S. Mouffe. University Park: Pennsylvania State University Press, 1978.

Higginson, Louisa. This manuscript diary of Thomas Wentworth Higginson's mother is in the collection of the Houghton Library, Harvard University.

Higginson, Thomas Wentworth. *Army Life in a Black Regiment.* Introduction by Howard Mumford Jones. Boston: Fields, Osgood, 1870. Reprint. East Lansing: Michigan State University Press, 1960. Most of this work is a revised version of the diary from the end of November, 1862, to the end of March, 1863; part is still in diary entry form.

————. *Diary.* 47 vols. MS in Houghton Library, Harvard University.

————. *Letters and Journals of Thomas Wentworth Higginson 1846–1906.* Edited by Mary Thacher Higginson. Boston: Houghton Mifflin, 1921. This work is almost unusable for the study of Higginson's diary because it contains only a tiny fraction of the original manuscript diary, and because it infrequently indicates which of its selections are from letters and which are from the diary.

Holmes, Sarah Katherine Stone. *Brokenburn.* Edited by John Q. Anderson. Baton Rouge: Louisiana State University Press, 1955.

James, Alice. *Diary.* Cambridge: John Wilson & Son, 1894.

————. "Alice James, Her Journal." Anna Robeson Burr. *Alice James: Her Brothers—Her Journal.* New York: Dodd, Mead & Co., 1934.

————. *The Diary of Alice James.* Edited by Leon Edel. New York: Dodd, Mead & Co., 1964.

McGuire, Judith. *Diary of a Southern Refugee During the War.* New York: E. J. Hale & Son, 1867. Reprint. New York: Arno Press, 1972.

Melville, Herman. *Journal of a Visit to London and the Continent 1849–50.* Edited by Eleanor Melville Metcalf. Cambridge: Harvard University Press, 1948. Melville's earliest extant journal.

————. *Journal up the Straits October 11, 1856—May 5, 1857.* Edited by Raymond Weaver. New York: Cooper Square Publishers, 1971. A fair travel diary of a trip to Greece, Turkey, and the Holy Land. A source for *Clarel* and several shorter poems.

Moran, Benjamin. *Journal of Benjamin Moran 1857–1865.* 2 vols. Edited by Sarah Agnes Wallace and Frances Elma Gillespie. Chicago: University of Chicago Press, 1949.

————. *Journals.* MS in Moran Papers, Library of Congress, Washington, D.C.

Myres, Sandra L., ed. *Ho for California! Women's Overland Diaries from the Huntington Library.* San Marino: Huntington Library, 1980. In addition to Helen Carpenter's record this book contains four other diaries.

Newberry, Julia. *Julia Newberry's Diary.* Edited by Margaret Ayer Barnes and

Janet Ayer Fairbank. New York: W. W. Norton, 1933. This diary of a rich young American woman who died of fever in Rome in April, 1876, is interesting in and of itself; but it seems even more fascinating as a parallel to and possibly even a source for Henry James's *Daisy Miller: A Study* published in 1878.

Ransom, John L. *Andersonville Diary*. Philadelphia: Douglass Bros., 1881. Reprint. New York: Haskell House, 1974.

Rosengarten, Theodore. *Tombee: Portrait of a Cotton Planter*. New York: William Morrow & Co., 1986. Includes the *Journal* of Thomas B. Chaplin, a South Carolina slaveholder.

Sanford, Mollie Dorsey. *Mollie: The Journal of Mollie Dorsey Sanford in Nebraska and Colorado Territories 1857–1866*. Edited by Donald F. Danker. Lincoln: University of Nebraska Press, 1959. The Pioneer Heritage Series.

Smith, Benjamin T. *Private Smith's Journal*. Edited by Clyde C. Walton. Chicago: R. R. Donnelly & Sons, 1963.

Stearns, Amos E. *The Civil War Diary of Amos E. Stearns, A Prisoner at Andersonville*. Rutherford: Fairleigh Dickinson University Press, 1981. Useful for a comparison with Ransom's diary.

Strong, George Templeton. *The Diary of George Templeton Strong*. Edited by Allan Nevins and Milton Halsey Thomas. 4 vols. New York: Macmillan, 1952.

Thoreau, Henry David. *Consciousness in Concord: The Text of Thoreau's Hitherto "Lost Journal" (1840–1841)*. Edited by Perry Miller. Boston: Houghton Mifflin, 1958.

———. *Early Essays and Miscellanies*. Edited by Joseph J. Moldenhaur and Edwin Moser. Princeton: Princeton University Press, 1975.

———. *H. D. Thoreau: A Writer's Journal*. Edited by Laurence Stapleton. New York: Dover Publications, 1960. An abridged edition.

———. *The Heart of Thoreau's Journals*. Edited by Odell Shepard. Boston: Houghton Mifflin, 1927. Reprint. New York: Dover Publications, 1961. An abridged edition.

———. *Journal*. Edited by Bradford Torrey. vols. 7–20. *The Writings of Henry David Thoreau*. Boston: Houghton Mifflin, 1906. Long the standard edition of the *Journal* and often reprinted, this edition is gradually being superseded by a new CEAA version prepared as part of *The Writings of Henry D. Thoreau* published by Princeton University Press, 1981–.

———. *Journal*. Edited by John C. Broderick et al. Princeton University Press, 1981–. This will be the standard edition, but at this writing only two volumes have been published.

Welles, Gideon. *The Diary of Gideon Welles*. Edited by Howard K. Beal. New York: W. W. Norton, 1960.

Woods, Daniel B. *Sixteen Months at the Gold Diggings*. New York: Harper & Brothers, 1851. Reprint. New York: Arno Press, 1973.

2. Other Materials

Bridge, Horatio. *Journal of an African Cruiser*. Edited by Nathaniel Hawthorne. New York: George P. Putnam & Co., 1953. Reprint. Detroit: Negro History Press, 1968.

Bright, Henry Arthur. *Happy Country This America: The Travel Diaries of Henry Arthur Bright*. Edited by Anne Ehrenpreis. Columbus: Ohio State University Press, 1978.

Hawthorne, Nathaniel. *Centenary Edition of the Works of Nathaniel Hawthorne*. Edited by William Charvat et al. Columbus: Ohio State University Press, 1962.

Herbert, Charles. *A Relic of the Revolution*. Edited by Rev. R. Livesey. Boston: C. H. Pierce, 1844. Reprint. Arno Press, 1968.

Inman, Arthur Crew. *The Inman Diary*. Edited by Daniel Aaron. 2 vols. Cambridge: Harvard University Press, 1985.

Moran, Benjamin. *The Footpath and Highway or Wanderings of an American in Great Britain in 1851 & 1852*. Philadelphia: Lippincott, Grambo & Co., 1853.

Thoreau, Henry David. *Walden*. Edited by J. Lyndon Shanley. Princeton: Princeton University Press, 1971.

SECONDARY SOURCES

1. Bibliographies

Arksey, Laura; Nancy Pries; and **Marcia Reed**. *American Diaries: Annotated Bibliography of Published American Diaries and Journals*. Vol. 1: *Diaries Written from 1492 to 1844*. Detroit: Gale Research, 1983. Vol. 2: *Diaries Written from 1845 to 1980*. Detroit: Gale Research, 1986. Supersedes Matthews's bibliography as the standard edition.

Matthews, William. *American Diaries: An Annotated Bibliography of American Diaries Written Prior to the Year 1861*. Berkeley and Los Angeles: University of California Press, 1945. Long the standard bibliography. Includes only a few late nineteenth-century diaries.

————. *American Diaries in Manuscript 1580–1854. A Descriptive Bibliography*. Athens: University of Georgia Press, 1974. An invaluable bibliography, but far from complete.

Meyerson, Joel, ed. *The Transcendentalists*. New York: Modern Language Association of America, 1984. An excellent bibliography of editions, manuscripts, and other research materials of the American Transcendentalists.

2. Other Materials

Baltzell, E. Digby. *Puritan Boston and Quaker Philadelphia*. New York: Macmillan, 1979.

Barrus, Clara. *The Life and Letters of John Burroughs.* 2 vols. Boston: Houghton Mifflin, 1925. Contains some journal entries not published elsewhere, including some dealing with his mother's death.

Bettleheim, Bruno. *Uses of Enchantment: The Meaning and Importance of Fairy Tales.* New York: Random House, 1976.

Burroughs, John. *Last Harvest.* Boston: Houghton Mifflin, 1922. Contains Burroughs's essay "Emerson and His Journals."

Cameron, Sharon. *Writing Nature.* New York: Oxford University Press, 1985. Cameron's study of Thoreau's *Journals* had only a limited effect on the chapter on Thoreau in this book because it was published just as this one was being readied for submission to the publisher. The finest work on Thoreau's journalizing, it is the kind of study on the diary as a literary form that I have long endorsed.

Channing, William Ellery, II. *Thoreau the Poet Naturalist. With Memorial Verses.* Edited by F. B. Sanborn. Boston: Charles E. Goodspeed, 1902.

Craik, Diana M. Mulock. *Life for a Life.* London: Hurst & Blackett, 1859.

Crews, Frederick. *Sins of the Fathers: Hawthorne's Psychological Themes.* New York, Oxford University Press, 1966.

Donohue, Agnes McNiell. *Hawthorne: Calvin's Ironic Stepchild.* Kent, Ohio: Kent State University Press, 1985. Includes long sections on Hawthorne's *English Notebooks* and *French and Italian Notebooks,* 218–64.

Duberman, Martin. *Charles Francis Adams.* New York: Houghton Mifflin Co., 1961. Reprint. Stanford: Stanford University Press, 1968.

Edelstein, Tilden G. *Strange Enthusiasm: A Life of Thomas Wentworth Higginson.* New Haven: Yale University Press, 1968. Devotes most of its attention to the early years of Higginson's career, but does a good job of structuring an examination of Higginson's diaries.

Hampsten, Elizabeth. *Read This Only to Yourself: The Private Writings of Midwestern Women, 1880–1910.* Bloomington, Ind.: Indiana University Press, 1982. Includes commentary on diaries of the frontier.

Harap, Louis. *The Image of the Jew in American Literature: From Early Republic to Mass Immigration.* Philadelphia: Jewish Publication Society of America, 1974.

Howarth, William. *The Book of Concord: Thoreau's Life as a Writer.* New York: Viking Press, 1982.

Hull, Raymona E. *Nathaniel Hawthorne: The English Experience, 1853–1864.* Pittsburgh: University of Pittsburgh Press, 1980. A biography of the period covered in Hawthorne's *English Notebooks.*

Kagle, Steven E. *American Diary Literature 1607–1800.* Boston: Twayne Publishers, 1979. Twayne's United States Authors Series #342.

———. *Early Nineteenth-Century American Diary Literature.* Boston: Twayne Publishers, 1986. Twayne's United States Authors Series #495.

Levine, M. Herschel. "Oedipal Views of the Jew in American Literature." *Journal of Psychology and Judaism* 3 (1978):102–8.

Matthiessen, F. O. *American Renaissance*. New York: Oxford University Press, 1941.

Metzdorf, Robert F. "The Publishing History of *Two Years Before the Mast*." *Harvard Library Bulletin* 7 (1953):312–13.

Meyer, Howard N. *Colonel of the Black Regiment*. New York: Norton, 1967. Biography of Higginson focusing on his career as a reformer and his military service covered by *Army Life in A Black Regiment*.

More, Paul Elmer. "Thoreau's Journal." In *Shelburne Essays: Fifth Series*, 106–8. Boston: Houghton Mifflin, 1908.

Nin, Anaïs. *The Novel of the Future*. New York: Macmillan Co., 1968. Reprint. Collier Books, 1970.

Rahv, Philip. "Dark Lady of Salem." *Partisan Review* 7 (1941):362–81. Reprinted in *Image and Idea*, 22–41. New York: New Directions, 1949.

Schlissel, Lillian. *Women's Diaries of the Westward Journey*. New York: Schocken Books, 1982. Includes material on several diaries including that of Helen M. Carpenter.

Shanley, J. Lyndon. *The Making of Walden with the Text of the First Version*. Chicago: University of Chicago Press, 1957. Examines the fashioning of *Walden* from Thoreau's journal.

Shaw, Peter. *The Character of John Adams*. Chapel Hill: University of North Carolina Press, 1976.

Spengemann, William C. *The Forms of Autobiography*. New Haven: Yale University Press, 1980. Although this work is concerned with autobiography proper it offers a great many ideas that can be applied to the study of diaries.

Strouse, Jean. *Alice James, A Biography*. Boston: Houghton Mifflin Co., 1980.

Tuttleton, James W. *Thomas Wentworth Higginson*. Boston: G.K. Hall, 1978. This biography focuses on Higginson's Transcendentalism.

Young, Philip. *Hawthorne's Secret: An Un-told Tale*. Boston: David R. Godine, 1984.

Index